THE WARRIOR'S QUIVER

On Earth as it is in Heaven

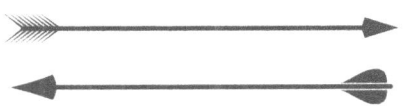

ANDREW MEYRICK

THE WARRIOR'S QUIVER: On Earth as it is in Heaven

Andrew Meyrick

Cover Painting created by Andrew Meyrick

Published by Seraph Creative in 2023

United States/United Kingdom/South Africa/Australia

www.seraphcreative.org

TABLE OF CONTENTS:

Acknowledgements   4

Foreword   5

Endorsements   7

Introduction   9

A Heaven to Earth story about us   17

Arrow One - Detachment from the Godhead   29

Arrow Two - Communication: How does God talk to us?   39

Arrow Three - A love affair in Heaven transferred to Earth   53

Arrow Four - The Garden: How does it grow?   59

Arrow Five - God's network: How we flourish and connect   71

Arrow Six - Watchers at the Gate   83

Arrow Seven - The Power of Oneness   93

Arrow Eight - The Power of Communion   99

Arrow Nine - The Baptismal Trinity and the gifts of the Spirit   115

The Bow - A resting Peace and Faith   121

Epilogue   135

ACKNOWLEDGEMENTS

I dedicate this book to my beloved wife, Elo.

She's not only help edit but also contributed majorly from her own intimate relationship with the Lord to the revelations and confirmations I received.

She has been a perpetual source of encouragement to step out of the "box" and link the word to the revelation. Her end notes in key areas in "Warriors of Love" and "Quiver" provide foundational proof of Yeshua being Spirit and the Word.

Without her Quiver would have ambled on as an incomplete work.

Thanks also to Doctor O my apostolic mentor and dearly beloved friend and family member on earth. To many others who have inspired me on Earth and in Heaven to travel on from warriors of love.

Especially Chris, Lindi, Linda, Lea Gary, Brian, Bob and John.

I hope you enjoy this next journey of revelations trying to bring Heaven to Earth showing where everything is finished before it even starts.

John 19.30

FOREWORD

Andrew and Eo are modern-day forerunners of the mystical coherence which unites every human living with an uncommon profound intimacy with the Living God. Since I met them, their every breath, word and gesture exude the Love of the Lord.

Their conversation is deeply rooted in the gospel yet finds relevance in the heart of every seeker of truth, a witness to their belief in the power of love. In this work all of these are interwoven, love of The God-The LORD and humanity. As their whole being exudes with this principle so this work pours forth the perfumed fragrance of the heart of the Father revealed in Jesus Christ and represented by their lives as Warriors of Love.

Adonijah Ogbonnaya
AACTEV8
Lake Elsinore, California

ENDORSEMENTS

I so enjoyed The Warrior's Quiver. Andrew's journey into the Father's Kingdom and subsequent encounters are beautifully written and encourage the reader to step into the same world by faith, with joy and with ease.

I highly recommend this book and know it will inspire you in your pilgrimage.

Lindi Masters
Ignite Hubs International

I met Andrew in the spring of 2019 and I was struck immediately by his clarity of thought and his courage to talk openly about our living, loving God all within a few minutes of our first conversation!

I have now read Warriors of Love and The Warrior's Quiver and the impact both of Andrew's books have had on the quality and depth of my Christian faith and my relationship with God has been profound.

In The Warrior's Quiver, I found Andrew's concept of "as in Heaven" not only fresh and thought-provoking but when you truly ponder on it, absolutely transformational!

In Warriors of Love, Andrew shares some of his incredible experiences and for the reader, this is so generous and valuable, most definitely adding to the richness of his books.

So, for an extraordinary experience and an opportunity to ponder on and deepen your Christian faith, I thoroughly recommend Warriors of Love and The Warrior's Quiver to everyone!

Alan Clark
Exponential Coaching Ltd

INTRODUCTION

Very truly I tell you, whoever believes in Me will do the works I have been doing, and they will do even greater things than these because I am going to the Father. And I will do whatever you ask in My name, so that the Father may be glorified in the Son. You may ask Me for anything in My name, and I will do it.
John 14:12-14 New International Version (NIV)

Following the publishing of the book *Warriors of Love* in June 2012, the Lord started to nudge me on another book. Then two people prophesied over me. They said another book was on the way and I would receive downloads from Him.

It was clear from inception this was going to be all revelatory. There would be some teaching, but the bulk would be matters He would be explaining to me for dissemination to the World and to His Body.

First, He took me back to the Lord's Prayer or better described as the Apostles' Prayer. "On Earth, as it is in Heaven...." He kept on repeating it to me like a mantra, so I would ingest and digest it.

This is Father's Kingdom as the prayer is addressed to God the Father. Kingdom means King's Domain (sphere, territory). If our task is to bring His Kingdom to Earth, that is fine. What He was reminding me of is that everything originated in Heaven. If we are thought of before time began by the Uncreated One, nothing on Earth, as it stands, is original. It all started in Heaven.

By looking at things from a Heavenly perspective we can understand more clearly why human thought and processes have developed the way they do. Sometimes it has taken years and years for things to become apparent and the revelation of its simplicity shines through. God makes nothing complicated. Everything He has planned and worked is perfect, efficient and purposeful. He is the Author and Finisher. We are part of the assembly line on Earth: Chapter 2, paragraph 3, for example. He has taught me this revelation about signs and wonders, healings and miracles. I do not need to know His plans. He just unfolds to me what I need to know when I need to know it and through obedience and intimacy, I do what I am told. His timing is perfect. Mine is faulty. He may bring healing to someone at a far slower speed than I would wish. He may delay a miracle. He works outside time with His angels. Man's challenges and errors have progressively detached him from the Godhead. He is striving, examining and learning in his own strength, not God's. This has been a major mistake.

> *"For My thoughts are not your thoughts, neither are your ways my ways," declares the Lord. "As the heavens are higher than the Earth, so are My ways higher than your ways and My thoughts than your thoughts."* Isaiah 55:8-9 New International Version (NIV)

I believe He is bringing in a new breed of men and women who listen to Him closely and learn Heavenly things that have never been revealed before. These people have attained the spirit of Sonship and spend much time with the Lord. They have an intimacy and friendship unattainable on Earth. They hunger for Him and lean on Him for advice and revelation.

Because these believers are trusted and obedient, they become open to revelations and mystical experiences, which allow them to see how Heaven is run and how the Godhead works. Love pervades all in Heaven, as it should do on Earth. Light takes out darkness. The latter starts to fade even with a flicker of a match. Those of you who have tasted Heaven will know what I mean. It is indescribable, all-embracing and one never wants to return to Earth. No epithet, aphorism, or adjective can describe God's unconditional love for us. Since He loved us first, we learn to love Him. It would be impossible otherwise. When we start to love Him then we learn to release His love through us to others. It does not stop here. He wants to instruct us and educate us in His ways.

This book is about that type of instruction. How we can receive it and use it for His Purpose.

I think we are entering a new phase in the end times where the full force and authority of the King of Kings is unleashed against the satanic remnant on Earth and in the dimensions of the Universe. He is beginning to use humans in a way far beyond their understanding to take down the principalities and controls of Satan. He is starting to reveal the truths of His Kingdom, that all emanated from Heaven in the first place.

Warriors of Love is a type of primer similar to school primers in Latin and Greek. It is a foundation tool for people to understand the importance of God's end-time army

'On Earth as it is in Heaven....'
He kept on repeating it to me like
a mantra, so I would ingest and
digest it.

and why we need to join it. I realise that the structure He gave me, models our Earthly armies. "As it is in Heaven." What a surprise! The revelation of the sequel of the book is just becoming apparent now to me in this book. I was already acknowledging, unbeknownst to myself, that everything did originate in Heaven.

FROM HEAVEN TO EARTH

For some time now, He has given me the gift of seeing angels but particularly worshiping angels. Why I wondered? My task was to introduce them to their earthly mortals who were musicians and worship leaders. This I have done obediently and with much hilarity and success. I will recount two cases later. The message He was giving me was that all inspiration and music for Christians came from Heaven in the first place. I am sure you can begin to see this. Where Heaven is impacting earth, Satan has always tried to

counterfeit and change this. Offshoots appear that are not Godly. All sounds, frequencies, and words come from Heaven. Worship angels guide and download musicians and songwriters inspired music and libretti for the glorification of their Maker. How amazing is that?

ORIGIN OF THE BOOK, The Arrows, Bow and Quiver.

As the Lord started to unpack the need for another book, He kept on giving me the words "a Quiver of Arrows." I realised that as a warrior, it was one of my weapons and arsenal. I had been given many prophetic words, long before I wrote *Warriors*, that I was a warrior and an archer in the Spirit realm. What was so special about this particular weapon instead of a sword or dagger or spear? Then it came out: "I am the Quiver; you are the arrows!"

This completely blitzed me for a few days. Well, a quiver is a vessel and yes, we use it to put arrows in. When He left earth to rejoin His Father, Jesus left the other part of the Godhead to guide, counsel and protect us on Earth: The Holy Spirit.

Quiver is also used as a verb: To shake with a slight, rapid, tremulous movement; to vibrate, and often with emotion. (Merriam — Webster) Does this begin to sound like the Holy Spirit? Yes.

If Jesus is the quiver via the Holy Spirit and we are His arrows, suddenly our purpose becomes clear. He fires us out into the world. We are safe inside the quiver, protected and ready for action. So many pictures present themselves. But then He said. "My warriors carry the Quiver (Me) and fire out My arrows at people!" So not only are we His arrows but we are obviously sending something out on the arrows that are not of us but of Him. This makes sense. On the point of the arrow is the arrowhead. The arrowhead or projectile point is the primary functional part of the arrow and plays the largest role in determining its purpose.

I insert a story of a picture given to a beloved sister of mine, which came to her one day in 2012. She had no knowledge of the book or of the title or the revelation I had received on arrows.

> *"While we were soaking at Prayer School today I had a picture of the Lord with a quiver and bow and He was somehow carrying lots of different substances around Him. Then He took the arrows, one by one, from His quiver and dipped each one in a particular substance, then fired it at each one of us, so that we each received from Him whatever we needed today. That was my impression of what He was doing. There was an impression of thoughtful purpose, but He was half smiling too!"*

Well, that was a good confirmation for me. Then came the blockbuster. He is the God of ambushes. That's why I adore Him.

I was "Googling" a "quiver full of arrows" and kept alighting on Jeffrey Archer's book. This gave me no enlightenment. Then, tucked below in the "search" on the screen was the verse, Psalm 127:4–5.

I looked up the verses to study them and their relevance. While I was absorbing these passages, my iPhone was playing music in my left ear. Out of one hundred and twenty-one songs of soaking music, guess what was being sung? The Sons of Korah, Psalm 127, verses 4-5

> *"Like arrows in the hands of a warrior so are the children of one's youth. How blessed is the man whose quiver is full of them; They will not be ashamed when they speak with their enemies in the gate."*

I burst into paroxysms of laughter and giggling. I reckon they were chuckling in Heaven too. "A coincidence!", the cynic would say. No, a complete God-Incidence!

There is no such thing as coincidence for the Believer. I was pretty convinced I was on the right track but the Lord gave me a final confirmation at a Church event a few days later, run by Holy Trinity Brompton (HTB). One of their last speakers, Jentezen Franklin, spoke on the topic of Gatekeepers and Archers and then launched into Psalm 127 verses 4 and 5. He even took out a toy bow to demonstrate the purpose of his sermon.

Having received the revelation and the extraordinary confirmations I started to process. The next revelation to arrive before I was even given a break, was that the book was the quiver, and the chapters were the arrows! This seemed pretty logical if the arrows were the revelations He wanted to share. As He was firing arrows at us in the Prayer School, revelations hit us all individually and were specifically targeted for each of us. So, what was He dipping the arrowheads into and what was the relevance of Psalm 127 to the simile of children? Jentezen Franklin said the children were our arrows whom we fired into the future thus bridging the generations. I think He was "spot on". In God's world, things can take on multiple facets and applications.

It was quickly becoming apparent He had a torrent of comparisons to give me that showed how everything started in Heaven and how we could relate earthly things to Heaven thereby gaining wisdom and understanding the conclusions.

> God makes nothing complicated. Everything He has planned and worked is perfect, efficient and purposeful

For a few months, the Lord has been taking me back to re-read *The Final Quest* by Rick Joyner, a revelatory first book of the trilogy published in 1996.

It is as relevant today as it was then in terms of prophetic visions.

As the warrior archers for the Lord climbed the mountain to avoid the hordes of demonised people, they fired arrows with purpose from various heights. Some hit their mark and sometimes they had no effect on wounding or terminating the enemy. Some were directed at Satan's own people and many at the captive Christians who had demons on them. Clearly, the choice of arrows was very relevant and at some heights and trajectories, the contents on the end of the arrow tip had a greater impact. Why? Each arrow had a different impact and success. The wrong choice, the wrong impact.

Types of bow:
Long Bow
Flat Bow
Cable Bow
Cross Bow

The most well-known bow is the long bow. One has recently been found that has been dated at 3500 years. This bow, which generally stood at 1.8 meters, was used in major battles by archers from the early centuries including the one hundred years war. One was used effectively by a British Soldier in WWII. The arrows can travel a great distance if the archer uses an arcing parabolic trajectory to his target.

And so the story begins. Jesus is the Quiver, the Vessel, we are the arrows, the Holy Spirit is the Bow, and the Archer is the Father who fired the first Arrow. (see John 3 verse 16)

A HEAVEN TO EARTH STORY ABOUT US

He who o/ercomes, I will make him a pillar in the temple of My God, and he will not go out from it anymore; and I will write on him the name of My God, and the name of the city of My God, the new Jerusalem, which comes down out of heaven from My God, and My new name.
Revelation 3:12

While finishing the book I felt the Lord tell me I had to insert the story of how Elo and I met. This story is going to be difficult to swallow for a lot of people, even born-again sons. Frankly, this does not worry me as I am just the messenger, as always, and readers need to engage in faith and trust and breathe in the Holy Spirit *Dunamis* to absorb the message.

Our God and His Son and Holy Spirit are the Creators of the Impossible in our earthly eyes. We are spirit beings, not earthly, and we need to walk in the spirit, in the hidden place that is often invisible to the naked eye.

When the Lord put Elo and me together he had already been preparing us fcr years for such a time as this.

I had been on the potter's wheel since 2004 when He ambushed me at my lowest point and manifested in my life. I received the full baptism of the Holy Spirit and Fire when least expected. I heard His words so clearly and what He said about me. I was totally undone in public whilst repenting after He gave me a glimpse of the Bema Seat, with video clips of my life with "pauses" from birth. They were clips I hated watching as they showed He had seen all I had done and thought. Nothing of what we do or say is hidden from Him.

In *Warriors of Love*, you can read how He honed me from a broken marriage (my fault) through to a seasoned Warrior, taking scales of "earthly dross" off me slowly and rushing me through a course of SEAL-like training.

He showed me the different "church" operations that had evolved around the world and why they so often failed. I knew I would never fit into many of these environments ever again as I was only to be used as a visiting messenger, healer, prophetic intercessor and watcher.

Yeshua gave me an apostolic mentor in Heaven (John the Evangelist/ Revelator) and one on Earth (Dr Adonijah Ogbonnaya).

Elo (my wife) also had an extraordinary preparation for her bridegroom. She had developed psychic talents at an early age by performing telekinetic actions, mind reading, and general alchemic activities that were not under the guidance of the Holy Spirit. When she was ambushed and saved, her powers were taken away for a considerable time for her to learn obedience, humility and righteous behaviour toward her God.

By 2013 I had already proposed to three beautiful women of God whom each accepted and then ran. I asked the Lord why. He said, "Andrew, I told you in 2010 I would present you your bride, but you could not wait. None of the ladies were presented by Me to you. Your purpose with them was to minister to them not marry them! But you did not ask me."

Humbled, I set off again and waited. In 2013 I saw a lady on Facebook who had two mutual friends whom I trusted as mighty men of God. This was a God incidence. I sent a friend request and she accepted. I received an amazing message on my site which knocked me over with supernatural resonance. We started to correspond for a week on Facebook messenger. Fifty thousand words later and a few Skype calls with this lady in South Africa and I was smitten with her spirituality, Heavenly knowledge and encyclopaedic memory of every verse in the Bible.

A few months earlier, I had a vision of myself seated on my Heavenly charger, Hineni, dressed in classic armour with a visor and sword and a massive regiment of angels behind me. Suddenly a dark horse, fully resplendent in body armour with a woman astride, galloped alongside on my right and kept my pace. Under her helmet she had long hair flowing. I knew instinctively who she was. She was the bride He was going to present to me at some point.

Now just to make sure we were aligned; Yeshua had given Elo a Heavenly horse a while back (to meet me). His name was Hashim and had no bridle! While she was riding, she had asked the horse why she had no reins or saddle. The horse replied, "Trust me, I know where he is, I know where I am going, and I know where to find him." (Hashim was alluding to me.)

So, the meeting was established in Heaven before the time began, for us to meet each other:

8TH MAY 2013, 12:43 PM, GMT SOUTH AFRICA

We were both joined in the Spirit as we were talking on the phone. I was in England and Elo in Boksburg, South Africa.

Suddenly Elo went into a vision. She saw the ancient Hebrew letters floating in the air — as if they were the anatomy or the atoms of existence. I closed my eyes and saw the same thing.

We both got blasted enough so that we fell off the surfaces we were sitting on.

Elo said to me, 'I am going up!" I said, "I am coming up too!" We were both sucked out of our bodies and next moment, without any apparent travelling, found ourselves in what appeared to be the Holy of Holies or like an anti-room to a bedroom. The walls were panelled with wood and the fragrance in the room was overpowering. We saw the Ark of the Covenant as well as the Mercy Seat on top and a Menorah and Oil lamps and gold writing on the wall.

I had decided to check we were really in the same place by asking her what she saw. I saw an eagle was perched on the left on a golden stand. I asked her to turn to her left, saying nothing and asking her what she saw. I did not want any auto suggestion.

Thankfully she saw the same eagle. We both turned to the right and were transfixed ...

In a high-backed seat with wide arms, we saw Yeshua looking at us leaning back and smiling.

One did not need to understand, one knew. The light pouring off Him was half blinding yet one could see His face and features and body clearly. He was in a cream robe with a sash of purple and a wide belt of gold. We were mesmerised by His sandals, and a very bright ring on His wedding ring finger. A blue purplish pulsing light jewel. Like an amethyst.

The Lord Jesus arose from where He was sitting.

While writing up the testimony we were given Revelation 1:13: "and in the midst of the seven lampstands One like the Son of Man, clothed with a garment down to the feet and girded about the chest with a golden band."

The Lord came towards us. We were at one moment standing gawping and the next, we were on our faces like John. A Revelation 1:17 experience.

After what seemed like a long time, I saw His sandaled feet before my eyes as He gently lifted us up to our knees. He laid His hands on us. He gave us our individual scrolls of a golden shade. I was given a belt — black and blue on either half or the robe of a king which was dark blue in colour.

An eagle came to sit on my right side and a dove on my left. The meaning of this being that I am an eagle in the Spirit and the dove (symbolic of the Holy Spirit) will refine and perfect my human nature.

Out of nowhere, a larger double-handed sword appeared in front of me. It had a beautiful handle, and the haft was inscribed in old Hebrew. Later I found out it said, "Holiness unto the Lord." (Zechariah 14:20-21). After our crowning ceremony in which Elo also received a golden sceptre, a crown and a brilliant white gown and a blood red robe, both she and I fell to the ground again.

We were still flat on our faces when Jesus again approached us. After remaining there for just a while, gazing at His feet and beauty, He helped us up, placed both of our hands in each other's and wrapped something round them, binding our hands to His. We were too taken aback initially by all of this to realise the meaning of it all: we were being married by Him!

Later He showed us how He had torn a perfect piece off from His seamless robe which He used to wrap our hands. He spoke for the first time and said, "Whom I put together no man will put asunder." He then asked us if we wish to stay a while longer and I said "yes".

"Follow me," He said.

We flew to a mosque in South Africa. It was an amazing trip travelling at high speed about a thousand feet up. We both asked the Lord, "What do You want us to do?" He told us, "To light the mosque with His Presence and drive out any and all demons that are there."

After having done that, we saw the entire building burning with fire. His fire. Our task was apparently complete.

We flew further, over fields of green with our Saviour and His squadron of angels being our protection. We took off into the sky and space. On and On through flashing channels and holes we sped. Yeshua was no longer with us.

I called out when I saw a massive wall of what appeared like a citadel ahead with turrets and a wide parapet. There was a cannon on the battlements. We floated up and landed on the parapet looking inwards. Yeshua appeared some way down the battlements and walked towards us.

He turned us around and said, "Look out beyond." Initially, we saw nothing but sweeping His right arm from low left to top right He cried, "This is My New Jerusalem!"

We looked out and saw an incredibly beautiful countryside. The colours were off the spectrum and creation, with every atom, could be seen in all the leaves, trees and water. Animals of all *species were roaming peacefully together. Valleys, mountains, lakes rivers. Overwhelming. Impossible to describe well.*

He then said to us, "You are my Watchmen."

We asked if we could stay but He said He wanted us to return to earth to tell the story.

Kingdom marriages start in heaven and come to earth.

He sees Oneness in a couple, the enemy sees only twoness.

We were to bridge generations (we were His Boaz and Ruth. We are 40 years apart in age).

He spoke Galatians 3:28.

The dead are all alive in Heaven.

We were to tell others that He is alive, that Heaven is real and that He would return.

The next moment we slid back with a jolt into our respective bodies. As we were both trying to get up from the floor in South Africa and the UK, Elo asked, "Do you know what has just happened? We have been married! It is sovereign!" I said, "I have not even proposed to you yet!" I did propose and Elo accepted!

Then it came out: 'I am the Quiver, you are the arrows!'

A couple of days later I was spoken to at 2:22 am and told by Jesus that the prophesy of Brian and the vision he had been given some time back was complete, that I would be presented with His Bride and not go searching any longer!

That word came in a Lie Bust session (a Sozo-style ministry) from Brian Trueman. Brian saw a vision in the spirit of me on a charger as "Warrior of Love" with a regiment of angels behind me.

A lone rider with long hair, on a black horse, came alongside me dressed in armour, a visor and a veil. I could not see the face. This was my bride being presented. Brian had not known about my vision.

> The Lord gave us Genesis 2:22, *"Then the rib which the Lord God had taken from man He made into a woman, and He brought her to the man."*

We asked the Lord about where and when to marry. He had been talking to Elo about the Feast of the Tabernacles for a while. We both got blasted as the word *Sukkot* came through and it became clear that this was the intended period for the marriage (end of September normally). We asked for the year, and He said this year, 2013.

Elo was given Esther 5:1–3 which gave us a day to calculate from Hebrew. He gave her the number 21. (It was 3 days after the 21st of September which was the length of fast that Esther had already completed and when she went to the King. She requested that Haman be invited to dinner. He was planning the destruction of the Jews. We believe we should fast for three days before the wedding on behalf of Israel.

We asked about the location. He said, "Israel." Where in Israel? Galilee. Then He gave us a choice: Capernaum in the hills or down at the lake. On the same day, I was praying with Brian who very firmly got Galilee too.

I asked the Lord why Capernaum? He said, "What are your names?" I said, "Lord, I am only Andrew." "No, what are your names?" I got quite irritated with Him and He told me to go off and think.

I suddenly remembered I had been adopted at three months old and only recently received the real birth certificate in full. I found it and it read: Peter John Jones. It was Andrew, Peter and John. "Now you know why I want you to go there. I picked up Andrew, Peter, and John on the beach!"

> Elo was given Matthew 4:18: *"And Jesus, walking by the Sea of Galilee, saw two brothers, Simon called Peter, and Andrew his brother, casting a net into the sea; for they were fishermen. Then He said to them, "Follow Me, and I will make you fishers of men." They immediately left their nets and followed Him."*

POSTSCRIPT

We encountered much opposition in getting Elo's visa to Cyprus from South Africa for the civil wedding. The Lord showed us a picture of us on a boat to Cyprus and adverse winds were slowing the progress. He took command of the weather and blew us back on the course putting a banner of love around the ship. The next day the visa, after three previous attempts, was released to us early morning in Pretoria.

We had our civil ceremony on the 9th of October in Nicosia, Cyprus, under perfect skies and heat. The Cypriot staff were delightful, and it was a very emotional and supernatural affair. The next day we set off for Israel.

We arrived in Tel Aviv with a new date, 16th October, and arranged for the earthly celebration to be held in Capernaum by the Lake of Galilee on a fishing boat called Faith. We had the Messianic Seven Blessings pray over us and said our vows on the Lake of Galilee.

It was an amazing event with much angelic presence as well as a cloud of witnesses and the Lord turned up too. Three very close friends came as well. We were able to plan a guided tour and visited the Holy Land and had many encounters wherever we went.

JESUS THE MESSIAH AND HIGH PRIEST — A FOLLOW-ON TO THE HEAVENLY WEDDING. THE TEARING OF GARMENTS.

One day, a fresh revelation came at 4:44 am about the garment of Righteousness; the price paid for our inheritance in Christ.

When the high priest rents his robes refusing and denouncing Jesus, he detaches the whole Jewish race from God. The only other robe not torn that day was Jesus's seamless outer garment. They cast lots for it. It represented the unity of the church. Jesus had torn His garment for us in the marriage to use as a unifying force.

The Lord just told us that the reason why His garment was not torn was because nothing could stop His garment from covering the nakedness of the people. He hung naked on the cross so that we could put on the righteousness of God.

He took us to Matthew 1:1, "The genealogy of Jesus the Messiah. The record of the genealogy of Jesus the Messiah, the son of David, the son of Abraham."

In the first line of the New Testament, the gospel writer affirms Jesus as the Messiah. This must stick in the craw of the Jews, whose Messiah He is supposed to be.

> *"Then Moses said to Aaron and to his sons Eleazar*
> *and Ithamar, "Do not uncover your heads nor tear*
> *your clothes, so that you will not die and that He will*
> *not become wrathful against all the congregation.*
> *But your kinsmen, the whole house of Israel, shall*
> *bewail the burning which the Lord has brought*
> *about."*
> Leviticus 10:6.

This was a clear warning about falsely tearing your clothes and denouncing God. God's wrath would fall upon the people. When the high priest rent his garments in front of Jesus, this was symbolic of two things.

The first was that he was rending his garments to signify the blasphemy he perceived Jesus has spoken. The priest had asked Him whether He was the Messiah. Jesus had replied, "I am." The priest did not believe Him.

The second symbolic act is that it is traditional that Jews tear their garments when somebody dies and it heralds the 7 days of mourning. The high priest, by tearing his garments and baring his naked chest, was acknowledging Jesus as a dead man for His perceived blasphemy.

The Lord showed us that in fact the priest who had not recognised the Royal High Priest before him had condemned himself to death for not recognising and accepting the true Saviour of the Jews. This act also condemned the Jews to separation from God.

It is not a coincidence that this happened at The Fall. When Adam and Eve sinned they recognised their nakedness and bared their chests in the same way, condemning themselves and the earth to death. They did not recognise the sovereignty of God and His message.

These two people, as the full embodiments of God, would have been representing King and High Priest. The Lord told me the high priest's role was to halt the works of the devil and Satan his minion. He had singularly failed. We have a choice to either have Jesus on our right hand or the devil.

> *"Set thou a wicked man over him: and let Satan stand at his right hand. When he shall be judged, let him be condemned: and let his prayer become sin. Let his days be few; and let another take his office."*
> Psalm 109:6-8 KJV

The high priest renounced his rights by listening to the devil. Caiaphas was replaced shortly after.

> The Lord then gave us this verse, *"There is neither Jew nor Greek, there is neither slave nor free man, there is neither male nor female; for you are all one in Christ Jesus. And if you belong to Christ, then you are Abraham's descendants, heirs according to promise."* (Galatians 3:28-29)

The high priest's action had opened the door for all to be saved and not just the Jews.

When we had our sovereign wedding and coronation by The Lord in Heaven, He reminded me of the linen He tore off from His robe to bind our hands with. He did it, He said, to show what God has put together, no man can put asunder. It represents the unity of the Bride and the Bridegroom.

Jesus as the Royal High Priest and King of Kings tore His own garment to bind our hands in marriage and it did not represent death. It represented resurrection and life. He said it represented the hands of God, the blessing of Elohim, the Creator of Heaven and Earth. He added, "My power is your power."

ARROW ONE

DETACHMENT FROM THE GODHEAD

This is about the arrow, which can be fired to bring back alignment.

> *"For I know the plans I have for you,"* declares the
> Lord, *"plans to prosper you and not to harm you,*
> *plans to give you hope and a future. Then you will*
> *call on Me and come and pray to Me, and I will listen*
> *to you. You will seek Me and find Me when you seek*
> *Me with all your heart."* Jeremiah 29:11-13 New
> International Version (NIV)

God had a purpose for creating us for His pleasure because He loved us first. He had only the best purposes and intentions for us. We were not intended to have anything other than Heaven on Earth. The fall ensured a disparity between Heaven and Earth. Adam and Eve were given dominion over Earth and in their unfallen state, they experienced Heaven. In their fallen state, they handed Earth over to someone else. Let's just imagine everything came off-kilter. Pain arrived, toil arrived, and emotions other than love arrived. In fact, lack and negativity arrived. We know who from: the proud and jealous fallen archangel Heylel, pride, vanity and Man's attempt to outdo God arrived.

Ever since that moment, Man's control of man took over and arrogance in our ability to do without our Creator commenced. The history of the chosen race, the Israelites, tells a story of disobedience, lack of focus and pride as well as idolatrous behaviour. When God moved the sphere out even wider encompassing the strayed progeny of Abraham, the Gentiles and all other races, we continued not to listen. We created our own faiths, worshipping the cardinal elements: Earth, Fire, Wind and Water, forgetting Who created these.

As we continued to detach ourselves from the Godhead, Satan who came to kill, steal and destroy moved in successfully everywhere. Kill does not just include killing people; it means killing ideas, dreams, aspirations, hope, and relationships, in fact killing anything positive. Steal does not just mean property, it means fortunes, countries, patents, concepts, beliefs, etc. Destroy does not just mean pulverise or reduce to nothing. It means living without dying, destroying images, impressions, thoughts, dreams, plants and trees. Illness that comes from Satan can curtail the destinies and futures of people.

TRUE NORTH VS MAGNETIC NORTH

One day I felt God saying to me, "I am True North, Andrew. The enemy is magnetic north." So, for believers, as you will see, the enemy needs little to deflect us. For the unbeliever, the enemy managed to reverse completely the polarity axis on Earth. So, the North became the South. The mystic, Ian Clayton, confirmed this latter revelation he received from the Lord to me recently. It makes utter sense as these unfortunate unbelievers are travelling in the opposite direction.

THE RHUMB LINE

As a sailor, having done many thousands of miles across oceans including the Atlantic, I not only have great respect for the elements but also for the means to get my bearings. When GPS fails and satellites are not available, a compass and sextant are necessary. A sextant is a tool of navigation used to measure altitude and enables one to determine his location and thus plot a course to travel. These are instruments that have been invented on Earth, but which come from Heaven. They have an earthly significance but also a Heavenly one. If we were created for a purpose, we have a destiny mapped out for us by our Heavenly Father.

This destiny is like a compass bearing. Due to the curvature and shape of the Earth this means that as we position ourselves further North of the equator, by keeping a constant compass bearing, the Rhumb Line distance will always be a little longer than if we don't correct our direction. A Rhumb Line is a line crossing all meridians of longitude at the same angle, i.e. a path derived from a defined initial bearing. That is, upon taking an initial bearing, one proceeds along the same bearing, without changing the direction as measured relative to true North.

The fastest route to the USA from the UK is the same for planes and ships; head towards the Arctic more and correct one's compass angle. The route is shorter than if one went straight across. That's why you always see Iceland below from an aircraft. Depending on where your journey starts and final destination, one needs to correct the compass in degrees. As we know, when we sail upwind, we are unable to point at the wind so the compass bearing changes regularly depending on how close to the wind we can sail. Through life, the Lord does not always take us in one direction. Like sailing we have to tack, changing direction to get to the mark, buoy or port.

The Lord's destiny for us, as He is True North, will never follow a straight path until we are on the last lap and very close. He needs us to keep aiming towards Him but take into account the distances we are from Him to correct for distractions and diversions. Remember the Rhumb Line is the simplest and most perfect solution but depending on where we are in the world is not always the fastest route. Now if the enemy is the magnetic north, what does he need to do to skew our direction? Very little. He only needs to bring us off one degree over a long trip and we are way off the mark. That is what the Lord has been warning me.

One day I felt God saying to me: 'I am True North, Andrew. The enemy is magnetic north.

I sincerely believe that originally true north and magnetic north were in exactly the same position on the Earth's axis and had no differences between them. When the Fall came, the enemy managed to take the Earth off-kilter away from the Light of the

World, the True North, and the Source of Creation. Many believe that in fact the axis of the world was reversed. Such that the North became the South. Notice how we even used the word "true" in this context when the navigators and astronomers realised how the world worked.

On ships and planes, compasses are gyroscopically stabilised and corrected to bring us back to True North. In some instances, big magnets are placed outside to correct major aberrations of magnetism. Such is the seriousness of the effect. Magnetism is being drawn to something. Magnetic North, I believe the Lord is telling me, is Flesh and Earthly things, True North are the spiritual and Heavenly things. In my prayer ministry, I am often called by the Lord to gyroscopically stabilise people who have come off their true compass bearing. I never really understood why. Now I do, one degree off after a three-thousand-mile journey is eight miles. The enemy needs to do little to cause this.

THE PLUMB LINE

What is a Plumb Line? It is a weight, usually, with a pointed tip on the bottom, that is suspended from a string and used as a vertical reference line. It is used in theodolites and steel tapes as well as ensuring the verticality of buildings with respect to the gravity of a point in space. "I am the Plumb Line and the Rhumb Line", He said to me. This is very significant because just as if we are off the Rhumb Line we can be off the Plumb Line from Heaven. The enemy will also try and take us out of the Plumb Line of Heaven. "Imagine the right angle", He said to me. "I am the right angle at 90 degrees to the horizontal. Down from Heaven and out onto your horizon." The enemy we know is not under the Plumb Line nor is he on the Rhumb Line. How do we know when we are off the right bearing and literally detaching ourselves from the Godhead? Simply, it won't feel right! I think the gut feel should be called "God feel". How would He feel?

Our moral compass is calibrated before time began by God. It is pure, unadulterated and feels right. Our golden compass drawn by magnetism, not from God feeds our pleasures and selfish earthly pursuits. It takes us off the beaten track. When we put man above

God, we know instinctively there is a risk: Short-term pleasure in exchange for long-term pain. God, we know, is short-term pain for eternal pleasure.

As children, we are pure, untainted and naïve, trusting, open and naturally receiving and giving love. He loved us first and children know it. One can immediately analyse the world's impact on a child by watching them. If trauma or unhappiness has affected them, it shows. If unconditional love and fun have been there from the start, it shines through. Their compasses seem stable, and they flow freely. Watch an adult affected by trauma, pain or despair. They are often rudderless, bobbing from one thing to another, without focus or destiny. They have no bearing in place to direct them to their destination.

Whilst in the middle of the Atlantic, many years ago, with about fifteen hundred miles to the nearest landfall, a pigeon alighted on our yacht. After a short break, it took off again in the direction of North Spain. We took its bearing and as near as we could estimate, it was flying to the nearest point of land! Amazing. It had an inbuilt compass clearly calibrated perfectly. Do we have the same? I believe so. It is probably underdeveloped in most humans. The magnetic field clearly has an impact on all species. We seem to be the one that has been taken off True North. The Daily Telegraph ran a fun article in 2008 about cows that point north when they are resting. Three thousand deer in the Czech Republic, when observed, did the same.

We know there has been much research done on our polar effect, in other words how we are affected by magnetic energy. But as the Lord recently showed us (myself and Elo, my wife) it is the other way around. We, by our actions, have a greater impact on the Universe and Heavens than the planets have on us. Why should we, as God's children created in God's image, be lower than the planets? We are either sons of the First or sons of the Last Adam. If God then cursed the ground after Adam's sin, how much more would He then bless the Universe by our righteousness in Christ working through us to bring Heaven to the Cosmos (Universe)?

In the Second World War, the limpet mine divers who swam

undercover in darkness to place mines on ships used compasses.
What is less known is the
tests that were done on them
by our services to ensure
they got there. They swam
up lakes under test in pitch
black and strong magnets were put on the side to see if they
were taken off their bearing. Needless to say, they were. Having a
stronger right or left leg flipper strength also had an effect! There
was much to cope with.

'I am the Plumb line and the Rhumb line', He said to me.

So, are we affected in the spirit and in the flesh by magnetic and
electrical forces? I think so. But this is not the case at all when you
believe that the planets have no effect on you. "As a man thinketh,
so it is" it reads in Hebrew.

> Then Jesus came to them and said, "All authority in
> heaven and on earth has been given to Me. Therefore
> go and make disciples of all nations, baptising them
> in the name of the Father and of the Son and of the
> Holy Spirit, 20 and teaching them to obey everything
> I have commanded you. And surely I am with you
> always, to the very end of the age."
> Matthew 28:18-20 New International Version (NIV)

If Satan can take us off the Rhumb Line and Plumb Line, what do
we need to do to get back on it? We know that Satan lies. So, if
we are in agreement with a lie, we will probably be off the Rhumb
Line. If we subjugate ourselves to man in any way, we are certainly
likely to be out of alignment with God's Plumb Line. Subjugation is
not the same as under authority. We have to decide at any point if
the authority under which we sit whether Church, state, company
or parents is abused or out of alignment with God's behaviour and
wishes. One acid test is if there is Love covering it. If there is not,
then it is an authority being abused. If it is a controlling authority,
it will be demonic. Beware of authorities where unelected officials
have their own agenda, which does not follow the general ethos of
the authority.

Read 1 Corinthians 13 to sense check Love:

CORINTHIANS 13 NEW INTERNATIONAL VERSION (NIV)

"If I speak in the tongues of men or of angels, but do not have love, I am only a resounding gong or a clanging cymbal. If I have the gift of prophecy and can fathom all mysteries and all knowledge, and if I have a faith that can move mountains, but do not have love, I am nothing. If I give all I possess to the poor and give over my body to hardship that I may boast, but do not have love, I gain nothing. Love is patient, love is kind. It does not envy, it does not boast, it is not proud. It does not dishonor others, it is not self-seeking, it is not easily angered, it keeps no record of wrongs. Love does not delight in evil but rejoices with the truth. It always protects, always trusts, always hopes, always perseveres. Love never fails. But where there are prophecies, they will cease; where there are tongues, they will be stilled; where there is knowledge, it will pass away. For we know in part and we prophesy in part, but when completeness comes, what is in part disappears. When I was a child, I talked like a child, I thought like a child, I reasoned like a child. When I became a man, I put the ways of childhood behind me. For now, we see only a reflection as in a mirror; then we shall see face to face. Now I know in part; then I shall know fully, even as I am fully known. And now these three remain: faith, hope and love. But the greatest of these is love."

If there are any missing parts, then it is not from God. Where there is an orphan spirit, there is no spirit of Sonship. They do not co-habit. The same with the fruits of the Spirit. If these are not included in a man or organization's thought processes, words and actions, they are most likely not to be from Him at all.

We, by our actions have a greater impact on the Universe and Heavens than the planets have on us

The Plumb line is a direct connection with God. Unhindered, free, loving, protecting and complete. Just as the plumb weight senses the gravitational force, we feel it when God's covering is over us. Just as a clear way ahead and total peace reigns in our direction as we rest in Him, we know if we are under the Plumb Line.

Before I move on to the next revelation arrow, the Lord wanted to make clear how the sextant and its purpose originate in Heaven. The sextant as mentioned before is an instrument specifically for finding our position from celestial navigation. One measures the angle between two visible objects; normally, the celestial object is the sun or star, and the horizon is known as the object's altitude.

What the Lord was saying is we bring the Sun down to the horizon for earthly purposes. He brings the Son (Sun of Righteousness) down to the horizon in the spiritual sense. Both give us a positional fix for where we are. The latter is the most important.

THE SKY IS NOT THE LIMIT

While praying, a friend of mine was given a message from the Lord that I needed to expand on the significance of the sextant and the skies above. She was given Matthew 16 v 1-4 for me to dwell on.

> *The Pharisees and Sadducees Seek a Sign*
> *"Then the Pharisees and Sadducees came, and*
> *testing Him asked that He would show them a sign*
> *from heaven. He answered and said to them, "When*
> *it is evening you say, 'It will be fair weather, for*
> *the sky is red'; and in the morning, 'It will be foul*
> *weather today, for the sky is red and threatening.'*
> *Hypocrites! You know how to discern the face of the*
> *sky, but you cannot discern the signs of the times. A*
> *wicked and adulterous generation seeks after a sign,*
> *and no sign shall be given to it except the sign of the*
> *prophet Jonah." And He left them and departed."*
> Matthew 16:1-4 New King James Version (NKJV)

ARROW TWO

COMMUNICATION: HOW DOES GOD TALK TO US?

This is the arrow of close engagement.

A crossbow is very effective for close-quarter fighting. We need to get close to the Lord and stay close. The further away we are, the more risk of inaccurate messages and comprehension.

When Jesus was returning to Heaven, He made clear that the Father would send a Comforter in the form of the Holy Spirit. We know He is a separate part of the Triune God Head. The Dunamis power of the Holy Spirit hovered over the void to create all. This power, like the bow itself, is where all power resides.

The wood used from specific parts of the Yew tree gives the bow the tautness and spring necessary so when the bowstring is drawn back it creates dynamic thrust for the arrow when launched. The early long bow probably released arrows at up to 100mph. Today, they can be released at 200mph!

When we release the Dunamis energy of the Holy Spirit it can reach its destination in seconds over great distances. A wave of an anointed hand can knock over crowds of people hundreds of feet away. When the Lord taught me to "boom" people, I found I could touch people close and thousands of miles away in seconds. All it required was to vision the target in the spirit and release the word.

In 2013, as I was getting to know my bride, I was in Sussex, and she was 9000 miles away with her grandmother sitting on a sofa in a house in Boksburg, SA.

Here is Elo's story:

All of a sudden, I heard the loud noises of fighter jets launching missiles and approaching their target. Me. As I waited for and then felt the impact, I was lifted off the sofa upwards about 6 feet in the air and landed unceremoniously on the floor. I was unharmed. Sitting down again on the sofa I looked at my grandmother who was aghast with what had happened.

"What happened to you?" She said. "Are you alright?"

I replied, "Yes Granny, I think Andrew has just boomed me from England!"

THE POWER OF HIS VOICE NEAR YOU.

"But the Advocate, the Holy Spirit, whom the Father will send in My name, will teach you all things and will remind you of everything I have said to you."
John 14:26 New International Version (NIV)

THE INNER AUDIBLE VOICE

I love Bobby Conner the "gentle giant" prophet who spends much of his time talking to God. One day, God said to him, "I talk to you the same way you talk to Me, Bobby!"

This is the inner audible voice people hear. Perhaps they fear they are talking to themselves. It's not a booming strange voice that comes back at one. The answers and questions are always logical and gentle as well as being loving. As we are Spirit-made men, He talks to us through the Spirit (Holy Spirit).

THE CASE OF THE WOMAN WHO WAS HAEMORRHAGING

Here is an example of my inner ear hearing God talking to me. I was also given an image.

In 2010, I was on a prayer ministry team at HTB for the Alpha International conference where we were praying with many pastors from all over the world. One of the members of the team came up to me and asked me to stand with her and pray for her daughter-in-law who was dangerously haemorrhaging in an ambulance on the way to the hospital. She was risking the early termination of a child. The Lord told me to reach out for the hem of His garment and I saw a vision of Him ahead of me and I reached out. I told the person that we needed to prophetically transmit this to her daughter-in-law in the ambulance.

Shortly afterwards, I was approached by the person with excitement, and she told me what had happened. The daughter-in-law had seen the vision in the ambulance and had reached out. Her bleeding stopped instantly, and she was healed. When she reached the hospital, she was in for a quick check-up and was released.

When we release the dunamis energy of the Holy Spirit it can reach its destination in seconds over great distances.

I had the honour and privilege of meeting her in 2012 where we reminisced over the amazing miracle of Love by Jesus. Tears well up in my eyes at the way He loves us all.

SPIRITUAL RESONANCE

This is a mysterious area that much has been written on especially by spiritualists, New Agers, Buddhists and Hindus.

Spiritual resonance is a resonating emotion understood by the mind, body and spirit. It is often experienced in the chest and solar plexus. I asked the Lord about this.

Well, the Plexus is a central place for a collection of nerve endings and electricity. Solar is the conversion of Sunlight (Sonlight) into electricity! Yet again the Son, the Light of the World, sends energy and transmits it to us.

I find these surges in my solar plexus that I feel at times are confirmations or injections of something into me. The punch I feel is completely involuntary and can be quite violent.

I have had intense heat enter my head at the top as I lie down.

There is no question God is communicating with me. What He is doing is not always so clear. When extra powers and gifts are given, this appears to happen.

Some people, when praying, have a limb of theirs start to shake. A left or right hand for instance. I find myself rocking backwards and forwards constantly when standing.

Dunamis is the energy and resonance of the Holy Spirit (divine wind) that hovered over the face of the waters at the beginning of time.

Given that we have polar energy and electricity affecting us, it is not entirely surprising we react to these power surges. So, shaking, falling down, laughing, tears, gasping and tight chests appear to have the same origin. The Uncreated One is touching us. In all these cases it is very difficult to be in control as it seems to have been handed over to Him.

Just as magnets can draw in and push away other magnets that are not correctly poled, so can we. This would begin to explain matters when someone is heavily loaded with the Presence of God on them; people around who are in a close orbit are affected. Some, due to a more synchronised resonance, are more affected than others. There is no doubt that at that moment if Love is coming off a heavily anointed person, the recipients receive it.

I particularly like to do what I call God or Holy Spirit hugs. My vessel or body becomes a transmitting agent of His incredible Love to the other person. It does not happen if I do not abdicate myself entirely to His purpose. So, if it is myself in the flesh, it isn't the same thing. If it is me in the Spirit, passing hope, laughter, love, appreciation or some other emotion, the person receives it.

Certainly, musicians, like guitarists, get resonance with chords on their guitars that vibrate in the air and sometimes cause them confusion as it is like two notes colliding. Even in healing ministry, some people believe that only by laying on hands, can someone be healed. This is not correct. Peter the Apostle's shadow healed people when he walked past them.

I have extended a hand from some distance and Jesus healed someone. I have held a hand relatively close and the person has felt the fire of the Holy Spirit. It's all about whether we are a purified vessel for Jesus to work through or not at the time. The key to successful healing in co-labouring with Jesus is complete faith that it is not us, but Christ in us and the Word. If we speak the Word in faith, people will get healed as Jesus is the Word.

Recently I had been spinning in dance and extended my arms, and two young men over three metres away fell over backwards. How does one explain that? I don't know. All I can say is His energy and *Dunamis* came cff me.

I saw this in action for the first time at Lakeland in 2008 when Bobby Conner, having playfully "zapped" to the floor all the three rows of seated elders on the stage, decided to turn his attention on the audience. He called out to a young man in a black t-shirt and shorts at least 10 metres from the stage. "Hey, you have some anointing!", he shouted. He then proceeded to hold his hand to his mouth and blow via the mike and directed his hand out as if to hurl something. The young man standing rows back proceeded to be bodily hurled backwards over three further rows collapsing with about ten other people laughing. What was the Lord allowing him to do? I don't know, but it was fun and I definitely wanted an impartation of this, which Bobby gave me later.

It's fun and laughter in Heaven and the angels, when they are around us, join in the fun.

Another man of God with an enormous anointing and great humility like Bobby Conner is Andres Bisonni. This apostle can sweep his right arm from left to right and back from the stage and hundreds and hundreds of people collapse in the Spirit like fields of wheat in a high wind. I feel in a way this is what happens with us. Heaven is colliding with Earth. We are just His promoter!

Many people have extraordinary experiences of massive vibrations in their bodies as if they are plugged into thousands of volts of power. During this time, they have downloaded information, revelations or just a sort of spiritual rewiring that goes on. A mystery of God, which one day, He will unfold. One thing is clear. All we have uncovered about communication on earth is that it has its home in Heaven.

There is an extraordinary finding that has been emerging over recent years that positive communication works, and negative does not. Talking to plants, vegetables, animals and humans, the same result emerges. Positive loving talk builds and causes fruit, the negative destroys rapidly. Does this resonate with the Bible's message and Jesus' teachings? The power of life and death is in the tongue! Your tongue to be exact!

God communicates in so many ways to us, and half the time we are not aware of it; through music and sounds, using physical artefacts, through repetition, by the voice and words.

John 14:26 New International Version (NIV) 26 But the Advocate, the Holy Spirit, whom the Father will send in My name, will teach you all things and will remind you of everything I have said to you.

He is Spirit and Word, and the Bible is one of His principal means of talking to us. To those well-tuned into His bidding, He gives specific verses. Sometimes He leads one to a chapter, verse, or book in the Bible to study. God clearly understands our doubts about whether something has come from Him. Therefore, He often confirms three or four times in different environments so that even with the cynic, the margin of coincidence or error becomes not even plausible.

The example in the Introduction regarding the Quiver and arrows is perfect. In *The Warriors of Love*, the story about the broken eggs and the amazing links with five different people puts the coincidence beyond challenge. Here He is communicating at different levels to different people. The one common denominator was everyone was listening and obeying.

HOW DO WE COMMUNICATE WITH HIM? HOW DO WE COMMUNICATE HIS MESSAGES FROM HEAVEN TO EARTH?

Prayer

This is just about talking to God in our way. It does not need to be formulaic. This can be speaking out, muttering, sub-vocalising or just in our spirit. It can be petitioning, brooding, framing, declaring, praising, loving, castigating, thanking or just in hope. We have to remember; He knows what we are going to say before we even say it so it pays to be brief or He may doze off!

Worship

This takes on many forms — dancing, banners, music, and Prophetic painting.

Dance

This is a very special way of communicating with the Godhead as there is clearly a personal and corporate role carried out by the dancer. Some time back, a group of us were being taught prophetic dance and we were shown many photos of people dancing. What was captured on the camera was extraordinary. There were orbs signifying angelic presence. There were shapes, colours and objects that were not from the person. Depending on what clothing the person was wearing, from time to time, the person corporeally seemed to be utterly transparent.

Then we were shown photos from space and other arenas. The similarities were not only uncanny but also staggering. God has placed these images everywhere. A photo of the human brain is replicated in a sponge at the bottom of the ocean on a reef. Constellations in the stars and some planet pictures mirror our flowers. He is communicating again to us the fact that nothing we have is original.

With dance, there is a conversation going on between God and the dancer and back, which sends the message of worship, praise and thanksgiving up to Heaven. It's a love affair. When I dance without banners, He often shapes movements before my eyes follow. They synchronise with the worship music being played and the tempo. The conversation is continued by Him in bringing in His Presence and anointing to the place where I am.

Corporate dance, which we performed, was immensely powerful as everyone flowed with the same movements. An anointing of such strength fell on the group, which came off the lead dancer depending on what they carried as anointing. If they strived, nothing came off. If they flowed with the Spirit, we all felt it.

Banners

Banners are flags that are used for worship. They normally range from half metre square to larger. The best material is silk of about 5 momme weight. Some banners are plain colours depicting a message.

White — purity
Purple — royalty
Red — Blood of the Lamb
Pink — redemption, love
Blue — sky, sea, calmness, a river of life, revelation

Silver — redemption
Gold — glory
Green — healing, life
Orange — freedom, warfare, fire, holy, glory
Yellow — redemption, renewal, hope

Then there are the multi-coloured banners that depict a special message.

I have an eagle banner with Isaiah 11:2 written on it with all the colours of the rainbow. It is a prophetic banner and has a very strong individual anointing. It represents the battalion banner that I lead as a Golden Eagle General in spirit.

I have also a pair of fiery asymmetric flame-coloured banners that release freedom and energy. Both are gifts from the Lord of Lords to me. The former is like my sword and is not normally allowed to be used by anyone else unless I ask permission from the Lord. The latter pair, I lend from time to time.

The properties of the eagle banner are extraordinary and are still unfolding. If I fly the banner over someone or place it over their head, they are immediately transported somewhere by the Lord. Sometimes it is just a flight with eagles or as an eagle. I have so many testimonies recorded; there is not enough room here to relate them all. There are people who have been taken around the world in space, to Heaven, way out into the Universe. There are some who have flown over countries they have never visited. Some are taken on missions to pick up items. The Lord is always communicating with them in one way or another. One person got the message he was to return to Africa for ministry. Another person was transported to Israel and Jerusalem to pick up a document and return to the UK, whilst cutting off a connection between the two countries that the enemy had created in the spirit. Some just rise up like eagles on the thermals and get amazing views of the earth from way up.

These are all living testimonies of sane people!

God communicates in many different ways. One person very recently lost the phobia of flying which she had from birth as the Lord took her to extremities of gravitational pull and settled her back gently anc flew around the Grand Canyon. Amazing! My first flight is recorded in Warriors of Love without my banner and that had an extraordinary story and message He wanted to give me.

Music

I truly believe that the notes and sounds we use all come from Heaven in the f rst place. Louis Giglio has succeeded in recording and showing the sounds that come from space. Even the heartbeat noise from a far-off constellation sounds like the heartbeat an unborn child hears in the womb. Perhaps that's why children love the sound of burbling, four-stroke Harley-Davidsons!

Musicians who perform in worship bands often experience sensations of heavenly occurrences. For some reason or other, the Lord has given me the gift to see some specific angels. If I look with my eyes at musicians playing the guitars etc. I often see an angel playing behind or beside them.

One good friend was dozing on a sofa after some very anointed playing. I looked to the right of him and a tall angel stood with a musical instrument, somewhat akin to a guitar with a spearhead on the end — possibly a warrior musician angel. The Lord told me to introduce him to my friend. Well, this took place under much hilarity as he bobbed around next to the angel unable to see him but definitely feeling his presence. Now Rob (my musician friend had had massive blockages in composing music for a long time and I believe the Lord wanted him to meet Bernard his angel, for the purpose of inspiration and new songs and music. This started to happen the next day. Rob was so besieged with downloads of music and libretti he needed almost to call a halt. They came at some of the most inopportune moments and have continued since.

Another worship leader at a church in London had already been introduced to his angel, but strangely one day, I was watching him in worship and the angel had changed completely! This one was dressed in sixteenth-century clothing with a doublet and a velvet hat, just like a minstrel. I asked the Lord why. I got the answer, "ancient music of the Church, played by lutes, lyres and mandolins." Very strange. I approached Phil after worship and told him his angel had changed. I explained why I thought the Lord had done this; to get him to write and sing old canticles and ancient church music. Phil looked at me for about fifteen seconds and then said. "Wow, that is extraordinary. I was in Lincoln Cathedral a few weeks ago and was sitting in the nave when the most beautiful music came out from behind the altar where the monks and choir would have sat. It was an ancient chant and music. I fell in love with it and wanted to compose and play some."

So, this explains why the Lord had changed the angel; to give him inspirational downloads. Wonderful!

I do not need to add much about how we connect with the Godhead when worship music is played or sung. The mystery is how some songs suit some people and others suit others. It's a question of taste, atmosphere and state of mind when people hear notes.

Prophetic Painting

This is one way the Lord communicates with us very powerfully. The picture can come to one like a vision to draw or paint.

The prophetic rainbow heart picture in Warriors of Love given to me by the Lord via the original artist has great significance to me personally. It commemorated a teleporting journey I made with Him and also a covenant He made with me. This is summed up by a friend who received a song for me that He sang to her. It included a reference to the rainbow heart. Here is the song:

Andrew, my shepherd son
Your rainbow heart like Mine
Beats with 4/4 time
Son of My womb
Son of My tomb
Son of My Dunamis Resurrecting Life
Every drop of your blood fused with Mine
Your heartstrings tuned in My time
My Love you know
You burn with My freedom and the sounds of My Light
Sweet son of My heart
Sweet son-song of My soul
Your very breath blesses Me
Your words are My joy
Your song is My deepest pleasure
You satisfy Me, Shepherd son
My Andrew

Subsequently, my friend Dawn when she saw the picture later for the first time wrote this:

Dunamis is the energy and resonance of the Holy Spirit (divine wind) that hovered over the face of the waters at the beginning of time

"Oh, the Lord reminded me of something last night about your rainbow heart painting! Do you remember when I asked Him for a song He was singing over you? The second line was 'Your rainbow heart like Mine', haha did you remember that? I had no idea you had such a painting or a dream about it :) Wow God :) Your rainbow heart is His covenant heart Andrew. There is none of the old left. Only Him. Only His rainbow heart is your rainbow heart. A faithful, covenant heart, that abides in His truth forever. You cannot fail Him. He will not let your foot slip :)"

When I read this, I choked up with the message. What is superb is how He has used two different people to convey His adoring feelings for me through two different mediums. The confirmation is again unequivocal.

Worship as an individual

Sometimes as people stand or kneel and glorify and worship the Lord of Lords, He communicates to them in very special ways. It is unique to the person.

As I bow low, I am often wracked with electric jolts in my abdomen. Some people shake or bob, some sway forwards and backwards. I talk about these manifestations in *Warriors of Love.*

ARROW THREE

A LOVE AFFAIR IN HEAVEN TRANSFERRED TO EARTH

The Long Bow is used here to fire the arrows. Although the Heavenlies are outside time, distances are immense. The Lord gave us a vision for a special reason, among our six senses. The imagination or image-making apparatus is very key for us to envisage things. We can travel in the spirit instantaneously and experience time elapsing.

As Elo and I were transported to the City of God from the Earth, the sensation of time going by was long and we felt and saw ourselves going through space and galaxies. When we had the initial part of the out-of-body experience, one moment we were on earth and the next moment in this room. It could have been next door, but it wasn't. I think the Lord was showing us different methods of travel in and outside Time. Our first journeying was overland on Earth at a few thousand feet. Our return from the New Jerusalem to Earth into our bodies was instantaneous, like being hurled with nothing in between.

So, our senses were used by Him in different ways. But each time we were being fired like arrows.

> *We love because He first loved us.*
> 1 John 4:19 (NIV)
>
> *The Lord appeared to us in the past, saying, "I have*

*loved you with an everlasting love; I have drawn you
with unfailing kindness."*
Jeremiah 31:3 (NIV)

Here is one very clear proof that things started in Heaven. Love was conceived in Heaven. This love is unconditional.

As humans, we have categorised love into two types: being "in love" and "loving". We have then divided "love" into two types: a conditional love and an unconditional love. Is this what God intended? I am not convinced. We definitely struggle with the latter behaviour. What went wrong and where?

> *God's Love and Ours*
> *"Dear friends, let us love one another, for love comes
> from God. Everyone who loves has been born of God
> and knows God."*
> 1 John 4:7 (NIV)

> *"The Lord did not set His affection on you and
> choose you because you were more numerous than
> other peoples, for you were the fewest of all peoples.
> But it was because the Lord loved you and kept the
> oath He swore to your ancestors that he brought you
> out with a mighty hand and redeemed you from the
> land of slavery, from the power of Pharaoh king of
> Egypt."*
> Deuteronomy 7:7-8 (NIV)

Our relationship with Jesus is supposed to be intimate and deep; an 'In Love' state.

There is no sign of conditional love here. No prerequisites are set down by God. He then went on to include all Gentiles. He sent His only Son to appropriate and cancel all sin, past, present and future, suffer a horrific death, open the door for us to salvation and return to Heaven to await His second coming as the Lord of Hosts at the end of Time.

How about this for a mind-boggling statement; Jesus speaking.

> *"Until now you have not asked for anything in My name. Ask and you will receive, and your joy will be complete."*
> John 16:24 (NIV)

There are still no conditions on His love for us. We know what we are supposed to do.

> *Love for Enemies*
> *"You have heard that it was said, 'Love your neighbour and hate your enemy.' But I tell you, love your enemies and pray for those who persecute you, that you may be children of your Father in heaven. He causes his sun to rise on the evil and the good and sends rain on the righteous and the unrighteous. If you love those who love you, what reward will you get? Are not even the tax collectors doing that? And if you greet only your own people, what are you doing more than others? Do not even pagans do that? Be perfect, therefore, as your heavenly Father is perfect."*
> *Matthew 5:43-48 (NIV)*

The only thing Jesus seems to set down for us as a condition is to be "unconditionally loving!"

THE BRIDE AND CHRIST: HUSBAND AND WIFE LOVE

Our relationship with Jesus is supposed to be intimate and deep; an 'In Love' state. This is the love we have for a man or a woman initially when we fall in love. A deep longing for being in each other's presence and proximity. It is spiritual, intellectual and emotional love all rolled into one. Sadly, it often wears off, but His request is that it should remain through thick and thin till the end of time or death whichever comes first. It is a love that looks through to the heart, forgiving everything and not even aware sometimes of physical appearance and ageing.

That is the Love God has set aside for a husband and wife. The only way to display this love on Earth is to have His heart in ours and ours in Him. We start to see through His eyes and hear through His ears. Looking at the core of an image created in His own likeness: Holy, Righteous and Perfect.

PRIME LOVE

Clearly, God has intended an overarching Love, which differs from a marriage love. It is the unconditional love that flows between friends, parents, siblings and strangers. It is the "love" spoken of in 1 Corinthians 13: an enduring foundational love that also weathers all storms. It still looks to the heart of the person and not the exterior. It only omits the deep physical and soul connection love of a husband and wife where they are made one. It is often very strong, spirit-to-spirit with great resonance.

> The only way to display this love on earth is to have His heart in ours and ours in Him. We start to see through His eyes and hear through His ears

The true Sonship releases the Lord's love. It is un-offendable, free, and overwhelming sometimes. Jesus is vulnerable like His Father is. He hurts before we hurt and laughs before we laugh. We need to be the same.

I can only begin to feel the anguish of His Father's love as He turned away from His Son when His Son questioned His ability to go through with the task set down by God the Father. Once in the Garden and then on the Cross. "Take away this cup!" and "My God, why have You forsaken Me?"

ARROW FOUR

THE GARDEN. HOW DOES IT GROW? THE DRESSING OF THE ARROW

Close-up work administered by the Lord with our permission.

We know that from Jesus' teaching, we are branches on the Vine. We should know that we need to be vine-dressed seasonally. Pruned and taken back, watered, and nourished by the Dresser.

Arrows are dressed very carefully by the bowman. The feathers need to allow the arrow to spiral in flight like a bullet or rugby ball.

The shaft must be of the right wood and strength and length to suit the bow. When t is perfectly designed it represents humility.

We are very much the same as an arrow needing dressing. The Lord cannot launch us into flight without the right substance and make-up. We need to travel down a very narrow defined trajectory or path. We cannot be buffeted by the wind but pierce through the elements whatever they are. We need to be able to cope with the *Dunamis* power of the bow.

The power of the Holy Spirit is limitless. Can we stand up in the storm or do we fall over easily? As a vessel, we need to be able to dispense His power without being also overcome by it. Through God's grace, we can also become the launchers of the arrows.

"Catchers" are often positioned behind people who are being prayed over. This is for practical reasons. If you plug yourself into a 13-amp socket in error, you do not fall back lightly. You are quite likely to be hurled across the room. It is no good being a catcher for the minister of the *"Dunamis"* if you cannot cope with the Presence

of God. I once was called into a session where the catcher kept on falling over each time. I have to admit, after 10 minutes I was finding it hard to stay up too, such as the *Ruach* being released in the arrows (Wind/breath) by the minister.

Remember the speed arrows can arrive at!

> *"Now the Lord God had planted a garden in the east, in Eden; and there he put the man he had formed. The Lord God made all kinds of trees grow out of the ground — trees that were pleasing to the eye and good for food. In the middle of the garden were the tree of life and the tree of the knowledge of good and evil. A river watering the garden flowed from Eden; from there it was separated into four headwaters."*
> Genesis 2:8-10 (NIV)

The life of man began in a garden planted by God in Eden. Eden means "delight" or "luxury" in Hebrew. Eden was, I feel in Heaven or a location where God was perhaps on Earth. This was their own garden. Adam was appointed head gardener to cultivate and keep it. A river flowed out of Eden through the garden and onwards. It was a garden of paradise. It split into four large tributaries and watered the Earth. The river according to Revelation 22 flows from the Throne of God. It seems that the Tree of Life bridges it.

Two mystics I know, believe they are also spiritual rivers representing the Heart of God and the four heart valves. Since God is Spirit there is an absolute logic in this. Again, it confirms " On Earth as it is in Heaven." Our hearts are supposed to be like His.

We are our own gardens and need to cultivate them. Just as He waters us, we are supposed to water and irrigate the Earth. The River of Life is supposed to flow out of our bellies. We need to bathe in it. (Ezekiel 47)

Adam was given dominion over everything on Earth. After the fall, Adam and Eve were expelled from the garden. They were placed on Earth. Sin had to be excised from this garden. A cherub and a flaming sword were placed at the Tree of Life to protect it.

"And the Lord God said, 'The man has now become like one of us, knowing good and evil. He must not be allowed to reach out his hand and take also from the tree of life and eat, and live forever.' So the Lord God banished him from the Garden of Eden to work the ground from which he had been taken."
Genesis 3:22-23 (NIV)

So, the man had gained knowledge of evil, which he was not supposed to have i.e., Godlike. We have to presume he knew what good was. He was banished to Earth properly. Had he remained in the Garden, the Tree of Life would have been exposed and contaminated and evil would have remained for eternity.

Again, we see all started in Heaven where the Tree of Life resides and the River of Life flows from. See *Warriors of Love* for revelations on the River of Life.

We should know that we need to be vine dressed seasonally. Pruned and taken back, watered, and nourished by the Dresser.

God allowed Satan into the garden for a purpose. He had given us free will. Satan represented rebellion and pride and everything that was counterfeit. Satan is a superb distorter of reality. And yet what God allowed into the garden was permitted to continue in our own "gardens and fields".

So much of God's imagery on Earth from Heaven involves gardening, pruning, sowing, propagating, growing, refining, cultivating, and watering. Just as He left temptation counterfeits and irritants in the Cosmos, so He has done on planet Earth. As above, so below. This is God's Divine Law of Correspondence.

Take for example the tares defined by the Online dictionary.

Any of various weedy plants of the genus Vicia, especially the common vetch.

Any of several weedy plants that grow in grain fields.

Tares an unwelcome or objectionable element.

It is not a great surprise to find that vicia are used in witchcraft and they are bitter to taste!

As most farmers know, these tares are so similar sometimes to the grain crops that they can only be separated at harvest time. They remain next to their healthy edible neighbours throughout the lifetime growth of the crop. This sounds uncannily like us when we try to lead a righteous lifestyle. The counterfeit is always there. The "flesh alternative." It is not even in a parallel universe but right next door. Satan plants his own followers alongside the righteous but they are often wolves in sheep's clothing so difficult to distinguish. The parable that Jesus told is identical as He describes the Kingdom of Heaven.

> The Parable of the Weeds
> "Jesus told them another parable: "The kingdom of heaven is like a man who sowed good seed in his field. But while everyone was sleeping, his enemy came and sowed weeds among the wheat, and went away. When the wheat sprouted and formed heads, then the weeds also appeared. "The owner's servants came to him and said, 'Sir, didn't you sow good seed in your field? Where then did the weeds come from?' "'An enemy did this,' he replied. "The servants asked him, 'Do you want us to go and pull them up?' "'No,' he answered, 'because while you are pulling the weeds, you may uproot the wheat with them. Let both grow together until the harvest. At that time I will tell the harvesters: First collect the weeds and tie them in bundles to be burned; then gather the wheat and bring it into my barn.'"
> Matthew 13:24-30 (NIV)

The power of the Holy Spirit is limitless. Can we stand up in the storm or do we fall over easily?

Now we see why He wants us to guard our hearts and our dreams above all else, for out of it flows the issues of life. When we are "sleeping" either spiritually or literally he (the devil) is going to imprint himself onto the waters of our existence that flows into the Universe without any question. Even without our permission. God has placed eternity in our hearts. Therefore, we have to guard these waters. One of these ways we guard our hearts is by wearing the armour of God.

Have you often wondered why the dreams you dream play out in reality? It is because dreams that are dreamt by us are powered into the Universe through the power of our soul. Sleep is a very deep meditative state we enter in which either the thoughts and purposes of God can be made manifest or the desires and ill intents of the devil can be brought through. Meditate on Scripture as you go to sleep, and you will see your dreams transformed and the world changed. We both, before we go to sleep, commit our souls to the care of the Holy Spirit and the angels to ensure that we remain in a supernatural bubble of protection only receiving what the Lord wants to give us. The devil is not called the enemy of our soul for nothing.

This verse shows how the Lord can feed us even when asleep. The arrow of revelation and instruction is fired into us and sealed permanently.

> *In a dream, in a vision of the night,*
> *When deep sleep falls upon men,*
> *While slumbering on their beds,*
> *Then He opens the ears of men,*
> *And seals their instruction.*
> Job 33:15-16

God has loved the garden since the beginning of time. Here is a beautiful poem by Dorothy Frances Gurney

GOD'S GARDEN

> THE Lord God planted a garden
> In the first white days of the world,
> And He set there an angel warden
> In a garment of light unfurled.
> So near to the peace of Heaven,
> That the hawk might nest with the wren,

For there in the cool of the even
God walked with the first of men.
And I dream that these garden-closes
With their shade and their sun-flecked sod
And their lilies and bowers of roses,
Were laid by the hand of God.
The kiss of the sun for pardon,
The song of the birds for mirth,
One is nearer God's heart in a garden
Than anywhere else on earth.
For He broke it for us in a garden
Under the olive-trees
Where the angel of strength was the warden
And the soul of the world found ease.

The first garden is Eden and the last stanza is probably the Garden of Gethsemane.

THE FIG TREE AND ITS SIGNIFICANCE IN EDEN AND ON EARTH

Witches use fig tree wood for making wands for divination. Another surprise. The fig has various connotations in history. It is an aphrodisiac. It resembles genitalia; an intimate part of the female anatomy when opened and the male part when left whole. In Greek and Latin, it means fig and vulva.

We know that when man became aware of his nakedness, he covered himself with fig leaves. Whether the tree of knowledge of good and evil was a fig tree, remains unknown. God commanded Adam and Eve not to eat of it or they would die, intimating therefore that they would normally have lived forever.

The fig symbolises fertility and Israel in the Bible. When Jesus told the parable of the barren tree and the exasperated owner, He was teaching patience and the need to feed the tree to produce fruit. If it does, it can remain, if not, it can then be cut down. (Luke 13 v6-9)

I don't think it is possible to paint a perfect picture of Eden though

I am sure God has given some artists prophetic insight.

The Garden of Earthly Delights painted in oils on wood is a triptych (three parts) by Hieronymus Bosch, a Dutch painter. It is a powerful depiction of Eden before the fall, after the fall and damnation. Painted around 1500 AD it can be found in the Prado Museum in Madrid.

The Garden of Eden is undoubtedly supposed to be a delight to the eye as are our earthly gardens today. To the untrained eye, the myriad of flowers, plants, shrubs, trees and ground cover present a dictionary of obscure Latin and Greek names with very esoteric pronunciations. To the senses in general, the different colours, textures, aromas and scents are sublime. They display the glory of God and His creative hand at work. We probably only get a minute sense and image of what the lush growth and vegetation were like in Eden. The New Jerusalem we saw is likely to emanate from the garden. The garden also had exotic birds and other creatures that Adam was given the task to name. If he had dominion then over all creatures, perhaps we have much more than we think now that Jesus has restored all for us.

God can certainly speak through any medium He chooses, including animals. Animals, birds and insects contain the presence of God in them as does every plant, seed and flower. I certainly talk to animals and birds when they are close.

Bobby Conner had a conversation with a little bird in his garden. God was speaking through the bird in the Spirit! Let's develop our senses to do the same.

A bird in my mother's garden was on the gravel drive very close some years back and looking at me forlornly. It turned its head and looked towards the bird's feed container. The nuts had run out. The message was clear: "Could you replenish it?"

Whether we have orchards, vineyards, landscaped gardens or plots, the creative process that God ordained is there before our eyes. A loving hand is well-received as it gently nurtures and touches His plants. They thrive under love and attention. No wonder the message is there for us to do the same to each other.

WATERING THE GARDEN

The River of Life is crucial to watering God's garden as well as our own garden that He has put in us.

He has been revealing many revelations about this river that flows out from the garden. The Lord had me paint a picture, which has been given at His request as a gift to Pastor Ian McCormack. It is in our first book, *Warriors of Love*. One reader had a revelation from this picture that delivered her a lie of the enemy that she had been in agreement with for 42 years. The picture depicts Christ in the river and the mountains in the distance. I felt He was painting Himself facing the mountains almost walking back up against the current. However, I am not sure what way the current was painted. The revelation she received was He was facing the current.

Once in a "flying in the spirit moment" lesson I was leading, a woman was taken to the River of Life and found herself backstroking effortlessly against the rushing current of the river. Backstroke was her favourite stroke. She was swimming towards the Source.

I asked the Lord why she was doing this, and He answered, "What do fish do Andrew?" They face upstream (the Lord) and swim against the current to maintain their position and be able to breathe. Exactly. They can't breathe going downstream. Then the revelation about salmon came.

Salmon are migratory fish that go to the source of the river up in the hills and mountains to lay their eggs and go downstream out to sea after. They return eventually to die at the highest point. They are tested and strengthened by their trip up through ladders and waterfalls and rest at the source to regain the power to go back out to sea. Fish feed and are nourished by what comes downstream towards them. Trout particularly eat different flies and grubs according to season and their locations. Much food falls off the elder trees that overhang the river.

In the River of God's presence, we are supposed to do the same thing. Feed, nourish and grow. The river provides everything like it does for the fish. One thing is needful.

I include here by kind permission of Jeannine Rodriguez-Everard of Images of Light (www.imagesoflight.us) The River of God's Promises Request given to her by the Lord.

In My presence, your garden of intimacy with Me is watered.

In My presence, you will find an increase. You will burst into life even in the darkest of times. You will be fruitful, and you will experience the momentum of My Spirit moving rapidly on your behalf.

In My presence, I will reveal My covenant with you to you and speak to you of your inheritance in Me and your destiny in Me.

In My presence, you are saved from the enemy who wishes to destroy you.

In My presence, you will discover gifts you had no idea were in store for you.

In My presence, signs and wonders will be released.

In My presence, the thirst of your soul and spirit will be satisfied. My presence will satisfy you when you're in a dry place. My presence is a place of provision, the place where I provide for your every need.

In My presence, I will remind you of your inheritance and I will help you drive out those things that keep you from receiving your full inheritance. This will enable you to embrace the destiny I have for you.

In My presence, I will encourage you to possess your inheritance.

In my presence, I will speak to you of the boundaries of your authority.

The river of My presence is where you will cross over into all of My promises.

In My presence, I will reveal to you the weakness of the enemy. I will tell you secret things and give you the encouragement you need to step into My promises.

In My presence, I will release miracles that will enable you to reach your destiny. Key to releasing My power through that miracle time and time again is to remember it, to savour it and to tell people what I've done.

The river of My presence is where you will have victory over the enemy and his tactics.

The river of My presence is where I will restore territory that has been taken from you.

In My presence, I will lead you in the paths of righteousness, for the glory of My name and to prove to you that I am Whom I say I am.

In My presence, you will learn what is pleasing because you will drink from the river of My pleasures; you will drink from the fountain of life and in My light, you will see light.

My presence is a place of refuge and strength and a place that will bring you gladness.

When you're in a place of captivity where the enemy has you bound, if you come into My presence, you will remember your destiny, the place I've called you to be.

And I will encourage you and give you the longing you need to get back on track.

In My presence, I will bring to life barren places in your heart.

In My presence, you will find peace. You will hear My voice and when you obey, My peace will be released to you and peace will flow from you like a river.

In My presence, your eyes will be open to the supernatural realm and My glory.

In My presence, supernatural experiences are released.

In My presence, your eyes will be opened to the people around you who do not yet know, My Son.

In My presence, healing and life are released.

In My presence, I will provide you with all of the spiritual food you need. Everything that sustains you is found in the river of My presence.

In My presence is where you are baptized and re-baptised again and again... where you surrender and receive new life from Me again and again.

In My presence, is where you're meant to pray.

In My presence, divine encounters with unbelievers are released.

In My presence, you find fruit, sweet food for your sustenance for your life. It's where you taste My goodness.

As a vessel we need to be able to dispense His power without being also overcome by it.

My presence is what's going to change the face of the world: My presence in you.

In My presence is where you see Me, where you see Me on the throne, sovereign overall, ruling overall and totally in control.

In My presence is the place from which you're meant to serve Me.

In My presence, My light is given to you, the light that dispels all darkness.

In My presence, you will learn how to rule and reign with Me. You will come to know that you know that you know that you are indeed seated with Me in heavenly places.

In My presence, you will receive all you need so that rivers of living water will flow from your heart to the world.

ARROW FIVE

GOD'S NETWORK AND HOW WE FLOURISH AND CONNECT

An archer with an empty quiver is no use to anyone. He needs to have the quiver full of arrows. Each arrow will have a different purpose that he has no vision of until he needs to use them. The arrows connect him with a target and these targets may be connected themselves.

> *'Jesus answered, "I am the way and the truth and the life. No one comes to the Father except through me.'"*
> John 14:6 (NIV)

One day the Lord said to me, "You're my PoP!" For a moment I was nonplussed until I understood He was speaking to me in IT language: Point of Presence.

Just as we receive all when we are in His Presence, we become His Point of Presence on Earth. Was the IT world aware of using a Kingdom Acronym? I do not think so. But of course, we believe we have invented everything on earth. What arrogance we have. Where on earth do we think our intelligence came from?

WHAT IS A POP-IN-IT LANGUAGE?

On the Internet, a point-of-presence (POP) is an access point from one place to the rest of the Internet (POP also stands for the e-mail Post Office Protocol; see POP3.) A POP necessarily has a unique Internet Protocol (IP) address. Your Internet service provider (ISP) or online service provider (such as Microsoft) has a point-of-presence on the Internet and probably more than one. The number of POPs that an ISP or OSP has is sometimes used as a measure of its size or growth rate. (source: Search Telecom.)

I like the Wikipedia description: A point of presence (PoP) is an artificial demarcation point or interface point between communications entities. It may include a meet-me-room.

A POP IN GOD'S LANGUAGE

I know I am a communicating entity and an interface point with other people. But for me to be a communicating point I need to be highly contactable and almost virtual. Herein lies the revelation of the World Wide Web that the Lord of Lords is creating. While we idolise the technology and the equipment and software that drives the Internet, little did we know what His purpose was to deal with a world of this size.

As He has planned all, before time began, He must be so frustrated that we are not picking up the vibes and hints about what intelligence and know-how He releases to us along the way and the real purpose of it.

Christians must start believing they are Spirit Men. We need to get this on our grid and have a clear reference. Either we accept the stories of Elijah, Enoch, Philip and even Christ that one moment they were there and the next moment they weren't or we are hypocrites to call the spiritualists witches.

An archer with an empty quiver is no use to anyone. He needs to have the quiver full of arrows

I find it fascinating that even in the Catholic Truth Society booklet on the priest and mystic, Padre Pio, there is a whole section on his bi-locating and it is rarely mentioned that Padre Pio carried the stigmata.

God's network works in the Spirit as ours works in the flesh. We need to understand we can engage with this spiritual network. He has work for us to do to hasten the end times.

ISP

Let's examine the ISP (Internet Service Provider). An Internet service provider (ISP) is an organization that provides access to the Internet. Internet service providers can be either community-owned and non-profit, or privately owned and for-profit.

Access ISPs directly connect clients to the Internet using copper wires, wireless or fibre-optic connections. Hosting ISPs lease server space for smaller businesses and other people (colocation). Transit ISPs provide large amounts of bandwidth for connecting hosting ISPs to access ISPs.

So, a service provider is a little like a home group or church. It houses different clients and individuals in the same place.

API

Gary Beaton, a beloved brother of ours, was told by the Lord one day that he was an API. Naturally, he asked what this meant. You are an Apostolic Prophetic Intercessor! Gary was prompted to look up the explanations on the web for an API.

An application program interface (API) is a set of routines, protocols, and tools for building software applications. Basically, an API specifies how software components should interact. Additionally, APIs are used when programming graphical user interface (GUI) components.

In other words, an API is a messenger that delivers your request to the provider that you're requesting it from and then delivers the response back to you.

As he pondered on this revelation, he began to understand the links. A prophet was a messenger. An apostle was sent out and was a networker delivering the message to the recipient. An intercessor has a key role as a builder, brooder and buffer in the Heavenlies. We are His software and an API acts as a link person from building something in creation on earth through to completion.

ON EARTH AS IT IS IN HEAVEN

THE SERVER

There is an irony about this title, which we call the apparatuses that run and hold so much data in the data centres. They almost represent us, as we serve our Lord and Saviour. Just as we are supposed to serve and help people, so does the indispensable server somewhere in the cloud Data Centre or in the ISP's building do the same thing sending out bits and bytes onto the internet around the world to different POPs.

As we attempt to be Christ-like, we need to remember His Words. "I came to serve, not to be served". He contains all the data and knowledge which we draw from to provide too.

EVERYTHING IN IDEAS AND CONCEPTS, EVEN PROCEDURES AND PROCESSES, ORIGINATE IN HEAVEN

I was lying in bed the other day and the Lord asked me if I wondered about my role in the company I was working for. I was the program director rolling out a massive ERP (Enterprise Resource Planning applications) SAP S4/Hana in a large group worldwide. Although I had experience doing this before I had never seen any Heavenly Link.

"What were the stages we went through?" He asked me.

Requirements (for design):
Build/ Configure
Develop
Test
Transport and Cutover (activities from old world environment to new and the limboid state between)
Go live (in the new world)

As I worded this back to Him, who knew already all things, He said: "Andrew, what process do you think we follow in creating anything including babies who come to Earth?" I was speechless and tearful at the revelation.

When He places Infinity in our hearts, man can do anything.

THE INTERNET. THE WORLD WIDE WEB.

I truly believe the Net is the way the Heavenlies function. We are linked by many connections to many locations. The more locations and connections each person is tied to, the more the possibility that God's Word will get out and reach far-off places. The way that Facebook and LinkedIn, the social networking sites, have been created allows public and private information transfer. It is feasible to limit data flow on all of them with the right settings.

God's Kingdom is something we try and look at from an earthly perspective. He sees it from a Universe perspective. Each planet, constellation and galaxy is part of a massive network with interlinks and connections. Although it is now believed to be 37 billion light years across in distance, it needs management just like Earth.

If we believe in angels and the structure that God has put in place through His Son Jesus on Earth, it is naive to think The Uncreated One has not got a structure in Heaven to run the Universe.

URL

URL, put simply, is an address. In computing, a uniform resource locator (URL) is a specific character string that constitutes a reference to an Internet resource. A URL is technically a type of uniform resource identifier (URI) but in many technical documents and verbal discussions, URL is often used as a synonym for URI.

To be on the Net with data pages, we need to have an address. This address is housed in a server in a data centre with space rented by an ISP. This is no different to us on earth having a postal address where we can receive letters and packages. This is normally our home and office.

Christians must start believing they are Spirit Men. We need to get this on our grid and have a clear reference

To be able to be found easily on the Internet, each church nowadays has a URL.

GOOGLE

People speak of Google as being Godlike in its omniscience and omnipresence. However, it would not exist without what God has allowed to be created as a platform for the dissemination of information. The data is created by man in the picture or written form and then posted. Google is definitely an engine for search provided and allowed by God. Google is a sort of Book of Truth from an earthly perspective.

The Lamb of God is opening the real Book of Truth with no counterfeits or fake news, now in end times. This contains all the Truth about God and His Universe creation.

Daniel was given access to it briefly and then told to close it and seal it. In Revelation, we see who opens it and releases the Truth.

> 'So he said, "Do you know why I have come to you? Soon I will return to fight against the prince of Persia, and when I go, the prince of Greece will come; but first I will tell you what is written in the Book of Truth. No one supports me against them except Michael, your prince."'
> Daniel 10:20-21 (NIV)

> "But you, Daniel, roll up and seal the words of the scroll until the time of the end. Many will go here and there to increase knowledge."
> Daniel 12:4 (NIV)

> *The Scroll and the Lamb*
> "Then I saw in the right hand of him who sat on the throne a scroll with writing on both sides and sealed with seven seals. And I saw a mighty angel proclaiming in a loud voice, "Who is worthy to break the seals and open the scroll?" But no one in heaven or on earth or under the earth could open the scroll or even look inside it. I wept and wept because no one was found who was worthy to open the scroll or look inside. Then one of the elders said to me, "Do not weep! See, the Lion of the tribe of Judah, the

Root of David, has triumphed. He is able to open the scroll and its seven seals."
Revelation 5:1-5 (NIV)

As we become citizens on earth of countries and persona grata, we are given access to "truths" from an earthly perspective. The big question is how much of this is counterfeit and controlled by the enemy?

In the same vein, as we become citizens of Heaven and true Sons of God, we are given access to Heaven's Book or Scroll of Truth where there is no counterfeit and no deception.

Psalm 139. I feel compelled to include this by the Lord as it embodies something so special about His relationship with us. It is not confined to the earth.

For the director of music. Of David. A psalm.

> *You have searched me, Lord, and you know me.*
> *You know when I sit and when I rise; you perceive my thoughts from afar.*
> *You discern my going out and my lying down, you are familiar with all my ways. Before a word is on my tongue, you, Lord, know it completely.*
> *You hem me in behind and before, and you lay your hand upon me.*
> *Such knowledge is too wonderful for me, too lofty for me to attain.*
> *Where can I go from your Spirit?. Where can I flee from your presence*
> *If I go up to the heavens, you are there; if I make my bed in the depths, you are there.*
> *If I rise on the wings of the dawn, if I settle on the far side of the sea,*
> *even there your hand will guide me, your right hand will hold me fast.*
> *If I say, "Surely the darkness will hide me and the light become night around me,*
> *Even the darkness will not be dark to you; the night will shine like the day, or darkness is as light to you.*

*For you created my inmost being; you knit me
together in my mother's womb.
I praise you because I am fearfully and wonderfully
made: your works are wonderful, I know that full
well.
My frame was not hidden from you when I was made
in the secret place,
when I was woven together in the depths of the
earth.
Your eyes saw my unformed body; all the days
ordained for me were written in your book before
one of them came to be.
How precious to me are your thoughts, God! How
vast is the sum of them!
Were I to count them, they would outnumber the
grains of sand, when I awake, I am still with you.
If only you, God, would slay the wicked! Away from
me, you who are bloodthirsty
They speak of you with evil intent; your adversaries
misuse your name.
Do I not hate those who hate you, Lord, and abhor
those who are in rebellion against you?
I have nothing but hatred for them; I count them my
enemies.
Search me, God, and know my heart; test me and
know my anxious thoughts.
See if there is any offensive way in me, and lead me
in the way everlasting.*
Psalm 139

Notice the words "woven" and "knitted"; so similar to a network. Notice the fact that we can go up to the Heavens. The "how" will be dealt with later. It indicates we can fly or go through the veil.

Above all, it shows an appreciation even then that the knowledge of God surpasses all understanding. If we are only using what is believed to be, one-fortieth of our brain, what were the other thirty-nine fortieths for? In the Spirit perhaps!

We are in this world but not of it.

As we are spirit man and nearly 80 per cent water we clearly have a role elsewhere Jesus makes this very clear to those who follow and believe Him.

> *"If you belonged to the world, it would love you as its own. As it is, you do not belong to the world, but I have chosen you out of the world. That is why the world hates you."*
> John 15:19 (NIV)

So, what happened when the veil was torn?

> *"At that moment the curtain of the temple was torn in two from top to bottom. The earth shook, the rocks split and the tombs broke open. The bodies of many holy people who had died were raised to life. They came out of the tombs after Jesus' resurrection and went into the holy city and appeared to many people.*
> *When the centurion and those with him who were guarding Jesus saw the earthquake and all that had happened, they were terrified, and exclaimed, "Surely he was the Son of God!"*
> Matthew 27:51-54 (NIV)

Whereas, before the Holy of Holies existed, in the ark of the Covenant, this was the only location for the Presence of God. Christ has now become the access point to God and Heaven. We can in essence in our spirit man go through the veil to access Heaven. We become portable Arks.

Either we accept the stories of Elijah, Enoch, and Philip and even Christ that one moment they were there and the next moment they weren't or we are hypocrites to call the spiritualists witches

This is only by Faith, the currency of Heaven!

In 2012 Culture Changers was set up by Hugh and Ginny Cryer in the UK; long-time warriors for Christ who led Vineyard Winchester for many years. They were taken out by the Lord, to a new place to live and set up a network of Christian leaders. They were given initially people to select to join and the first meetings set the ground for nodal connection. Obedient and submissive to the Lord they followed instructions to the letter. I was honoured to be invited although I did not lead a church.

At one meeting one of the leaders was requested by the Lord to unravel a ball of string by rolling it out from himself to someone on the opposite side of the room. This then progressed haphazardly all over the room creating a sort of cat's cradle or web of connections. What nobody expected was that the inner core which had an end to it started to unravel simultaneously!

The upshot was double strands in all directions and quite messy.

It produced a revelatory picture of what God was doing by connecting people. He realised that connections would be distant at times and cross-referencing but He is clearly tired of churches within walls. He wants common links and attributes like on the Internet with no special favours or idiosyncratic behaviours. No eclectic or privileged closures. One way or another we were all connected. There was no real hub, there did not need to be. He was the Hub.

ARROW SIX

WATCHERS AT THE GATE

"And the watchers of the gate called and told it to the household of the king, within."
2 Kings 7:11 Rotherhams Emphasised Bible

As we begin to understand that all on Earth emanate from Heaven, our spiritual gates need protecting. The fact that we are, in effect, an Ark of the Covenant carrying the Holy of Holies, Jesus Christ, means that we are the watchers of our own bodies against invasion. The Internet, computers and IT work the same way.

Our bodies are like temples, citadels or cities. They have defences around them and access points. Like the Heavenly City, there are walls and on the walls, there are watchers. Watching for signs of attack.

We have an immune system. A cleansing system. This is covering the physical side of our Persona. We are however spirit beings first and our body is like a piece of clothing over the spirit so we can be seen. The Bible makes reference to watchers at the city gates. Their role is to warn of impending arrivals outside the gates and check if they are friends or foes.

We have physical gates, soul gates and spirit gates. The outer layer is physical. Eyes, nose, ears, mouth and our hands, and feet to sense and feel.

The inner layer is emotions, heart intellect etc. and the innermost is the spirit which is the connector with God via the Holy Spirit, the third person of the Trinity. If the outer two layers have gate entrances that are dirty or blocked, the person will never experience the Heavenly things on earth or operate in the glory.

"Who may ascend into the hill of the LORD? And who may stand in His holy place? He who has clean hands and a pure heart, Who has not lifted up his soul to falsehood And has not sworn deceitfully. He shall receive a blessing from the LORD and righteousness from the God of his salvation."
Psalm 24:3-5

We are supposed to be walking arks hosting God's presence. The world has done much damage internally and externally to most people due to Satan's dominance in their lives; choosing flesh over spirit.

The enemy is a beaten wreck and entity in the spirit if we only knew it. When we operate from the spirit, we are invincible. When we operate in the flesh we are not operating with God. God is spirit.

Just as attacks come against our flesh, some overt, some covert like viruses, so in the spirit and soul, we are attacked more subtly.

The Lord showed me through IT examples and the similarity with our bodies. As everything originated in Heaven they are staggering. It is ironic that watchers exist by default in IT.

A computer is generally fitted from inception with anti-virus software using the same name we use in our bodies.

VIRUS

A virus invades a computer's software and attaches itself to applications or even the operating system and can have dire effects as everyone knows. It can remain undetected for long periods. It can be triggered to activate at a date or point in time or through an action by the user. Hundreds of new viruses are created every day by mischievous hackers and perpetrators, sometimes for fun and some as cyber warfare to bring down systems. It can only be started by human action and like our viruses can spread and infect other computers on a network. The anti-virus software acts as a gatekeeper and watcher and tests inbound emails or downloads or cookies. The latter is a means to track people's movements around the web. Your computer has many cookies sent to it each day dependent on which sites you go visit. The excuse by the site owners is to track how many visits you make to them and gather marketing statistics. Sometimes it is more devious, to gather information about your habits.

WORMS

A computer worm is a standalone malware computer program that replicates itself in order to spread to other computers. Often, it uses a computer network to spread itself, relying on security failures on the target computer to access it. Unlike a computer virus, it does not need to attach itself to an existing program. Worms almost always cause at least some harm to the network, even if only by consuming bandwidth, whereas viruses almost always corrupt or modify files on a targeted computer.

TROJANS

The Trojan Horse is a malware software that coins its name from the wooden horse that looked like a gift but turned out to be a ruse and allowed the Greek soldiers to enter Troy inside the horse and take the city.

We are however spirit beings first and our body is like a piece of clothing over the spirit so we can be seen

It is now time to pause and reflect on the spiritual equivalent that the enemy uses to invade us.

A wolf in sheep s clothing is a Trojan horse. Someone who purports to be a friend but turns out to be otherwise. Pornography and lewd pictures and suggestive items are always used to justify our needs. Those who offer drugs and strong drinks to entice people further and break their inhibitions before exploiting.

Just as the watcher at the gate looks down and vets the person entering we need to do the same thing with everything we ingest through our ears, eyes, nose and mouth. Just as a virus detector needs to be kept up to date with new versions and upgrades, we need to do the same thing with our lives. If a computer has out-of-date software, it protects against old viruses but not against new malware.

People can be carrying spiritual viruses that infect others. A generational curse is a form of virus or a lie that someone says. It can replicate and be passed on to others. It can be handed down. These all come from being in contact or agreement with something that does not come from God.

FIRE WALLS

God is surrounded by fire. Computer networks are surrounded by supposedly impenetrable firewalls that block incoming attacks. Sometimes there are three layers. The missiles either disintegrate or bounce off these walls or are contained and examined. There is an irony that God has given the Israelis the "firstborn on earth" in His eyes, the Iron Dome, the mobile, all-weather air defence system. An amazing firewall to protect them.

> *"For I, declares the Lord, will be a wall of fire all round her and I will be the glory in her midst."*
> (Speaking of Jerusalem)
> Zechariah 2:5

The enemy is a beaten wreck and entity in the spirit if we only knew it.

We need to have the same systems set up to defend ourselves. We need advanced radar and early warning systems that notify us of changes in the atmosphere or circumstances or sentiments. Our physical bodies have these firewalls in place with immune systems. When they weaken, colds and viruses break out. We need spiritual firewalls, the Lord tells me, that is just as robust to protect us.

IMMUNITY TO ATTACK

> *"They will pick up snakes with their hands; and when they drink deadly poison, it will not hurt them at all; they will place their hands on sick people, and they will get well."*
> Mark 16:18

I cannot speak for others but for some reason or other The Lord keeps on giving me more forms of the ordinance. I have bouncing damn busting bombs, hand grenades, pints of Wigglesworth, shots of Godka and Mark 16 v 18 injections and flying flags. This may sound quite bizarre and from an earthly perspective, it sounds highly amusing. The results, when used, are varied depending on the person, the environment, the resonance and what exactly the Lord wants to do with people. I never try and second guess.

In most cases, I receive these supernatural tools by impartation from someone who is instructed to give them to me or I receive them directly. In almost all cases I receive a verse totally independent from the revelation. In effect to link *rhema* with the *logos*.

One case came as a total surprise in two portions. First the command and then the verse above. I was watching a person being prayed over by her parents whom I knew well. I always wait for instructions from the Lord before launching in. She had been leading worship and I sensed The Lord telling me to wait and do something shortly. I saw she needed refortifying in the spirit. It was very clear. He then suddenly said, 'Give her an injection/inoculation." I stopped in my tracks wondering what He meant but realised it was supposed to be a prophetic action. I didn't immediately ask about the content.

I went up to the lady and asked her if she was afraid of injections. The answer was negative. Relieved I explained what I had been asked to do. She smiled at me and agreed.

I proceeded to do everything a nurse or doctor would do. I pinched the skin lightly, applied some "warriors of love anointing oil" on the spot and proceeded to inject her with the syringe. I did this with all seriousness and love and compassion not knowing quite what the contents were or what the outcome would be. I trusted the Holy Spirit.

The result was extraordinary. No sooner had I withdrawn the "syringe", she collapsed to the ground where she stayed for some time. Neither my friends nor I had any idea what He was doing. It was not our affair or business. He was ministering. I got the giggles and so did they. Frankly, it's quite bemusing but I have gotten used to these rather bizarre activities as He has shown me before that Heaven is full of fun, laughter, love and joy so this is part of the package. If you carry Heaven on earth, expect to have fun. If you are not, you should be wondering where it's coming from as it's not coming from Heaven.

Soon after, I was given the verse Mark 16:18 above to confirm the reason why I had been given the right to administer. He sees us not just as barristers with briefs that He gives us but also as doctors and physicians in the spirit. He knew anyway I had always wanted to be a doctor from a young age. He had already allowed me to use the palm of my hand as a defibrillator to save someone who stopped breathing. This was just another tool.

Why were we getting an immunisation kit? It is against viruses, colds, attacks from warlocks or curses. The verse makes clear that He wants His troops to have morphine painkillers and preventatives whilst at war.

He has been teaching me about working from lack. I come across many Christians who bemoan why they are being besieged by illness and spiritual attacks when they are supposed to be covered by the blood of the Lamb and protected completely. Herein lies the conundrum.

At what point does one open the door to the enemy being able to sift? Best look at my book *Warriors of Love*. I Believe it is the moment one opens a door to a belief or action that does not come from God. Doubt, fear, unbelief, anger, frustration, in fact, anything negative will open the door. This makes a very long list. It is why it is better to ask to be judged each day and not wait around trying to guess where we stand. It's certainly not a good idea to wait till Judgement Day.

Jeremiah 17 v 9 and 10 are clear about who can judge and who can see what's going wrong. We are certainly not capable of doing this ourselves. We are too close to the issue.

DIPLOMATIC IMMUNITY

He gave me this phrase recently one early morning. I feel it has much to do with the continued review of types of immunity He gives us.

Diplomatic immunity is for members of the government and also for representatives of the Queen or Monarch when they are outside the realm in other countries. It ensures they are only judged under the laws of their realm and not others. There is the famous "diplomatic bag or pouch" to which no foreigner has

Just as attacks come against our flesh some overt, some covert like viruses, so in the spirit and soul, we are attacked more subtly.

access legally including customs and border guards. Secret papers are carried within these bags of communications between overseas embassies and their government and monarch. There are many stories of diplomats being smuggled out incognito during difficult times. Clearly, He is reiterating the fact that all this started in Heaven and the way the universe should run is similar. What came to be used on earth came from there. It is up to us now to discern from Him what has any counterfeit in it that does not have His seal on it.

If we try to maintain immunity from judgement or prosecution when we are not really acting on His behalf, we will be in trouble. If we glorify our exploits when we are not with Him, yet quoting Him, He will not know or recognise us.

ROYAL COURTS AND COURTS OF JUSTICE

> *"The angel of the LORD gave this charge to Joshua: "This is what the LORD Almighty says: 'If you will walk in obedience to me and keep my requirements, then you will govern my house and have charge of my courts, and I will give you a place among these standing here."*
> Zechariah 3:6-7

THE COURTS OF THE LORD — BOUND BY LOVE

Entering the gates of the Highest: Access denied to non-believers:

> *"Enter into His gates with thanksgiving, And into His courts with praise. Be thankful to Him, and bless His name."*
> Psalms 100:4

We have found recently that by following the Lord's instructions on declaring this verse daily and going through the veil to the courts that amazing things are happening. N.B these are not law courts.

He did of course promise us but it is so encouraging to see His results come through. He is always faithful, and our faith must look through God's eyes, not ours, which always have limited understanding.

As Os Hillman the author wrote in TGIF about the woman, whose son is dead, talking to Elisha: she knew something more than the current circumstances. She remained calm and expectant as she knew Elisha's God could resolve everything if He wished. He always wishes we praise and thank people including God whom we love. When we bless, we cover things with happiness.

He said to us one day, "I don't want you to be bound by Law but to be bound by love." So don't be bound by the tangible, legal constrictions of life. Be bound only by love.

ARROW SEVEN

THE POWER OF ONENESS WITH HIM

The steps to glory
It's all about Oneness and unity
Identity in Christ as a son
Unity in the body of Christ
Unity in community
Unity in marriage
Transformation of towns and cities happens
Peace comes
Restful soul remains
Freedom stays
Glory arrives
The steps to Babylon
It's all about independence and self.
Identity in self and icons
Disunity in the body
Disunity in community
Two ness in marriage
Disintegration happens
Total lack of peace
Total restlessness of soul
Captivity to addiction money and
state control
Hell on earth
I am in the earth but not of it.
A sort of alien from Heaven.

God's plan since Eden has been to bring us back into perfect relationship with Him.

GOD'S PLAN: THE END GAME IS ONE-NESS

The maturity of the church is coming:

> *"[That it might develop] until we all attain oneness*
> *in the faith and in the comprehension of the [full*
> *and accurate] knowledge of the Son of God, that*
> *[we might arrive] at really mature manhood (the*
> *completeness of personality which is nothing less*
> *than the standard height of Christ's own perfection),*
> *the measure of the stature of the fullness of the*
> *Christ and the completeness found in Him."*
> Ephesians 4:13 (AMP)

God's plan since Eden has been to bring us back into a perfect relationship with Him. When we have this relationship right with Him, we then can have the right relationship with our fellow men. Man's plan has been to override this by establishing a relationship between man and man. God has either been excluded or used as a medium to control other men. God and His plan will win. The Priestly Order of Melchizedek is being restored and these mighty followers of God will walk in the power required to bring God's blueprint to earth with no distortion or manipulation.

This is what is coming back now. The Garment of Righteousness and no longer the garment of shame that Adam and Eve acquired following the devil and not God.

Jesus was in the line after the Order of Melchizedek. He was not in the line of the Priests of Levi. He was a King and Priest. The four faces of Melchizedek will manifest blended into the four faces of Christ.

Lion — King
Ox — Priest
Eagle — Prophet
Man — Apostle

The priestly order of Levi is dead. Many will see the light and move into the Holy Spirit's power and authority. The rest will be blessed, but just not achieve the fulfilment of their destinies on their scrolls.

"The people of this Order will walk in great authority, power, and purity, leading God's people to higher spiritual levels of maturity and fruitfulness." (Quote from one of Nita Johnson's books)

HOLINESS IS RETURNING

The explosion in evangelism was needed to reveal Yeshua to mankind — Jesus' plan will only be accomplished through these people rising up (and not without hardship and suffering.)

My beloved had an open vision last night of Jesus sending special forces from Heaven who were being deployed out of helicopters everywhere to help the start of the End Time harvest.

The Lord had just said, "They are the SWAT team of salvation."

From when Time began we were planned to be in God's likeness and image and cocooned in His Glory. This is what is coming back now. The Garment of Righteousness and no longer the garment of shame that Adam and Eve acquired when following the devil and not God.

THE SONS OF GOD ARE RISING

"For [even the whole] creation (all nature) waits expectantly and longs earnestly for God's sons to be made known [waits for the revealing, the disclosing of their sonship].

For the creation (nature) was subjected to frailty (to futility, condemned to frustration), not because of some intentional fault on its part, but by the will of Him Who so subjected it — [yet] with the hope

That nature (creation) itself will be set free from its bondage to decay and corruption [and gain an entrance] into the glorious freedom of God's children. We know that the whole creation [of irrational creatures] has been moaning and groaning together in the pains of labor until now.

And not only the creation but we ourselves too, who have and enjoy the first fruits of the [Holy] Spirit [a foretaste of the blissful things to come] groan inwardly as we wait for the redemption of our bodies [from sensuality and the grave, which will reveal] our adoption (our manifestation as God's sons)."
Romans 8:19-23 (AMP)

ARROW EIGHT
THE POWER OF COMMUNION

1. THE SUPERNATURAL BLOOD TRANSFUSION: REVERSING THE AGEING PROCESS BY INGESTING THE LORD JESUS' BLOOD

Many of us have always wondered what physical benefits the Gospel of the Lord Jesus Christ has.[1] Now, due to teaching that has not been given in context, and goodhearted believers "lending their ears" to almost every apparent "minister" out there, a lot of tares have been sown into our doctrine causing us to believe that it is erroneous to ask such questions.

It's the job of every follower of Jesus to "test the spirits" as to see whether they are from God.[2] No matter how old the doctrine is. No matter who said what. We are commanded by the Lord to test the spirits and guard against the doctrine of devils. A subtle form of idolatry takes place when teachers replace the Word and Spirit of the Highest God. None are above reproach — not even the greatest and most admired teachers of this time. The Spirit and the Word always go together in this case. Be not followers of men first, but of Christ![3]

> It's the job of every follower of Jesus to "test the spirits" as to see whether they are from God

We were asked by the Lord to look at Psalm 103 and read through it until we found a verse in which He had given us enough "substance" to write an article about.

> *"Who satisfieth thy mouth with good things; so that thy youth is renewed like the eagle's."*
> Psalm 103:5 (KJV)

"Look up the meaning of the word 'satisfy' in Hebrew," we heard Him say.

שָׂ ב עַ / שָׂבַ ע

('saba' 'sabea' saw-bah', saw-bay'-ah) A primitive root; to sate, that is, fill to satisfaction (literally or figuratively)

Now, if we were to read the verse in the proper English whilst still maintaining the originality of the Hebrew language included, it would read like this:

"Who fills your mouth with good things; so that your youth is renewed like the eagles".

As we can see — there's a link between "youth rejuvenation" and the Lord "filling our mouth with good things."

We felt impressed upon our spirits to ask Him what "these good things were which causes our youth to be renewed by eagles". His answer amazed us to put it lightly. "It's My Blood and the Body" He replied. "Science will confirm this fact. After all, I am the One Who created the concept. Research the benefits of blood transfusion." He winked at us.

Hurriedly, we searched the Web and found an article in The Telegraph newspaper published some years back on Vampire blood therapy.

As we read through the article the Lord reminded us that He was the vessel through which all things were created. Naturally, everything points to Him. Finding Him, in all things, is gaining wisdom and understanding.[4]

We as Christians need to embrace the scientific aspect of the Bible as well but use discernment in order to recognize truth from deception. Use the "chuck it/park it" principle with the Word and Spirit as your foundation.

Here is a summary in point form about partaking of the benefits of Holy Communion through faith in Jesus Christ as your Lord and Saviour [Suitable for both men and women]:

1. Supernatural age reversal — the more you drink the Blood, the younger you'll become.

2. For the disappearing of spots and wrinkles.[5]

3. The ability for women to conceive and become pregnant at ANY age — with or without any age reversal. Remember Abraham partook of the bread and wine? He would surely have offered the same to Sarah as well.[6] [Jesus said: "If you do not partake of My Blood and Body, you have no life IN you"].

[Question: Do babies reside INSIDE of the woman?]. My godly advice is honour God and gets married first before even considering doing this. Love God and honour His commandments.

4. Partaking of it releases the elixir of life and allows you to become more like God.

5. It emits a portion of divine energy — helps to get you alert without your daily "coffee fix".

6. Gives you a blessed marriage.[7]

7. Displaying and having the FULNESS OF GOD manifest in your life.[8]

8. Increases the virility of a man. According to Jewish customs without it, the marriage would be childless.

*Remember excluding the cause of men becoming more manly, using your virility is meant ONLY FOR MARRIAGE. Keep the marriage bed holy are His instructions. Grace does not mean compromise.[9] Abstinence has its benefits. Of that, you can be sure. ;)

9. For signs and wonders, strength, and fertility.[10]

10. Healing.[11]

11. When all else fails, the Blood never will. Not in any case or circumstance![12]

12. Causes you to bear much fruit — in all aspects of your life.[13]

13. You receive the "Divine soul of the Lord" and achieve soul maturity.[14]

14. You become wiser.

15. It helps you to abide in Him and bear all the fruits of the Spirit.[15]

16. A man's potency increases.[16]

17. You increasingly gain the mind of Christ.

Let this realisation of HOW GOOD GOD IS empowered you to repentance and live a life full of His glory. You are NO LONGER UNDERNEATH ANY CURSE! ON EARTH AS IT IS IN HEAVEN![17]

References:

1. Psalm 103:21 John 4:1; Hebrews 5:14; John 5:41 AMP

2. 1 Corinthians 11:1; Romans 8:14

3. Colossians 1:16-17 NIV; 1 Corinthians 15:46; Proverbs 13:20

4. Eph 5:27

5. Gen 14:18; John 6:53; Josh 24:15

6. Col 2:9

7. Col 2:9

8. Heb 13:4; Rom 6:1-2; 1 Jn 2:15

9. John 15:5; John 6:56

10. Is 53:5

11. Rev 12:11

12. John 15:5; John 6:56

13. Gen 3:22; Heb 5:14; Lev 17:11-14

14. Gal 5:22; John 6:56; John 15:5

15. Gen 14:18; John 6:53

17. Matthew 6:10; Romans 2:4 AMP

*Keynote: Most of the Scriptures were taken from the King James Version Edition.

2. THE POWER OF COMMUNION - COMMUNION AND RESURRECTION

On Earth, as it is in Heaven.

While we were both meditating on the Name of God one day a while back, I placed a piece of unleavened bread into my beloved's hands as her eyes were closed. She suddenly opened her eyes saying she had felt a shift in the atmosphere!

When we inquired of the Lord what had happened, He told us:

"Sons have the right to choose how things will be on earth as it is in Heaven."

When Yeshua was on the earth and confronted with a dead relative He chose the outcome of this relative's fate which resulted in his resurrection. Lazarus came back to life because the Son saw there was no death in Heaven.

3. THE UNTOLD STORY OF THE POWER OF THE BLOOD: IT'S ALL IN THE BLOOD

Pondering at communion one day on the power of the Blood of the Lamb.

Remember the young children who are beheaded in Iraq whose parents had brought them up in the faith of the Lord Jesus Christ. They valued their lives little as they knew they were already resurrected. They preferred to not renounce their faith.

> *And they overcame him by the blood of the Lamb and by the word of their testimony, and they did not love their lives to the death.*
> Revelation 12:11

> *"Now after the death of Joshua it came to pass that the children of Israel asked the Lord, saying, ‹Who*

*shall be first to go up for us against the Canaanites
to fight against them?' And the Lord said, 'Judah
shall go up. Indeed, I have delivered the land into his
hand.'"*
Judges 1:1-2

4. THE PASSOVER ACCORDING TO THE BOOK OF EXODUS

As we continued our investigation into the Blood, The Lord told us to get back to the beginning of the Bible and meditate on Genesis 1 v 1 because in the beginning we will see it is all about the Passover and the Body of Christ.

We were taken to:

*"Now in this way you shall eat it: your loins girded
and your sandals on your feet and your staves in
your hands. And you shall eat it with haste — it is
the Lord's pascha."*
Exodus 12:11 Septuagint

*"And thus you shall eat it: with a belt on your waist,
your sandals on your feet, and your staff in your
hand. So you shall eat it in haste. It is the Lord's
Passover."*
Exodus 12:11 NKJV

He highlighted the phrase, "loins girded."

He asked us to look up other verses that contained this phrase particularly in the Old Testament. This led us to:

*And the hand of the Lord was on Eliou, and he
girded up his loins and ran in front of Achaab to
Iezrael.*
1 Kings 18:46 Septuagint

*Then the hand of the Lord came upon Elijah; and
he girded up his loins and ran ahead of Ahab to the
entrance of Jezreel.*
1 Kings 18:46 NKJV

He asked us to look up the meaning of: "Loins girded" In both these verses.

This was the way that people were used to travelling over rough ground, often at speed, as their robes would have impeded them. In effect bundling them up around their girth.

"Sons have the right to choose how things will be on earth as it is in Heaven."

He asked us to also look at "the hand of the Lord" and what it meant in 1 King's 18:46 (above), Exodus 13:3 and Exodus 12:41.

> *Then Moses said to the people, "Keep remembering this day in which you came out of Egypt, from a house of slavery. For by a mighty hand the Lord brought you out from there. And leaven shall not be eaten.*
> Exodus 13:3 Septuagint

> *And Moses said to the people: "Remember this day in which you went out of Egypt, out of the house of bondage; for by strength of hand the Lord brought you out of this place. **No leavened bread shall be eaten.***
> Exodus 13:3 NKJV

> *And it happened after four hundred and thirty years that all the host of the Lord went out from the land of Egypt during the night.*
> Exodus 12:41 Septuagint

> *And it came to pass at the end of the four hundred and thirty years — on that very same day — it came to pass that all the armies of the Lord went out from the land of Egypt*
> Exodus 12:41 NKJV

The hand of the Lord means with the "power of God", in other words, supernatural speed and force.

Just as Elijah shot forward at incredible speed so were the Israelites translated to safety. The journey from where they were to the Red Sea was over three hundred miles. With probably close to a few million people it would have taken a few weeks. They went overnight out of the land of Egypt!

The Lord mentioned He used a "portal" to us which makes sense. In fact, for the Egyptian army to be pursuing, even if the Israelites did dawdle and hang around by the sea, the soldiers would have likely with Pharaoh, gone through a demonic portal to catch up.

Now to the beauty of why they had to take the Host.

THE KEY IS COMMUNION

> *Jesus said to them, "Very truly I tell you, unless you eat the flesh of the Son of Man and drink his blood, you have no life in you."*
> John 6:53

"This is my body."

He is the Sacrament. "The fundamental sacrament of the Universe" (Dr Ogbonnaya) Remember Yeshua was crucified/slain before the beginning of Time. His body/host was sacrificed. We are made in the image of God and therefore become sacrifices as well.

The Israelites, before they escaped from Egyptian soil, took "communion" in their Pesach meal. They were not allowed to drink the blood of the sacrificed lamb only unleavened bread. Leaven raises the dough and represents pride and false doctrine.

> *"'How is it that you do not understand that I did not speak to you concerning bread? But beware of the leaven of the Pharisees and Sadducees.' Then they understood that He did not say to beware of the leaven of bread, but of the teaching of the Pharisees and Sadducees."*
> Matthew 16:11-12

Unleavened represents humility.

They took communion "the body of Christ" without being aware of it. By ingesting His body, they fulfilled Colossians 2:9 receiving for a moment the fullness of His Deity as we do.

The hosts of the Lord were the army of Israelites. Little did they know it (The Lord of hosts — Jehovah Tsebaoth) allowing them to be translated by flight (Those who wait upon the Lord will mount in wings of eagles).

> *"For in Him all the fullness of Deity dwells in bodily form."*
> Colossians 2:9

THE MEANING OF PESACH (PASSOVER) ANALYSING THE HEBREW LETTERS

Phe — Opening, an entrance.

Samekh — The number 60, a way, an aid, where Heaven touches earth. Ergo a portal. Six is a man and 10 is Yeshua God, the fullness.

Cheth — Inner room or chamber, Holy of Holies.

So, taking the Host, in communion, gives one an entrance to go through a portal to the Holy of Holies to experience the fullness of Yeshua the Christ or anointed One.

By the Israelites taking the Pesach they experienced an element of the fullness of God and His mighty Hand (earth heaven earth).

4. THE CONSUMED BODY OF CHRIST AND THE NEW BLOOD COVENANT

More Revelations on Communion and Praise and Thanksgiving

When we take Communion, we are taking the "consumed by fire" Body of Jesus. The Jewish Matzoh recipe specifically requires the singeing, browning and blistering of the baked bread and not the burning. We know that Jesus represented the burnt offering that replaced the cooked Lamb in the Passover meal. It's as if they only got half the message, which of course is the case. They believe there is a Messiah. Their error was not to have recognised Him when He arrived.

In the meantime, feast on the living fiery Sacrifice of our Lord.

When Jesus died on the Cross, the Blood flowed out of His Body into the earth with the water. This was when the Body and the Blood were divided.

At the Last Supper, He held up first, the bread, Manna from Heaven representing His Body. His Body was the living sacrifice broken in pieces and given to us. It dealt with sin and death.

The wine representing His Blood as it separated from His Body was the new and everlasting covenant or Will that is read at His death. It represented Life. It had to be separated as an undertaker and embalmer separates the body from the blood with us at death. If not, the blood corrodes.

There is life in the blood as we know. Our bodies cannot function without blood. Ergo that is why we have everlasting life from His Blood because He was resurrected.

CONCLUSION

If you don't get touched and anointed and refilled and renewed when you take Communion, you should be wondering if you are just going through the motions.

Kris Vallotton said he found himself doing this with the commissioning of 2000 Bethel students. Bless him for his humility and honesty. We need to be "in the Now" and "I Am" when we take Communion as it's a very intimate one-on-one, face-to-face common union with our Saviour.

In the meantime, the Kingdom is within us and strengthened by taking Communion regularly.

> *"But I say to you, I will not drink of this fruit of the vine from now on until that day when I drink it new with you in My Father's kingdom."*
> Matthew 26:29

It will be a new Blood and a new Body into which we fit.

> *"Now when He was asked by the Pharisees when the kingdom of God would come, He answered them and said, "The kingdom of God does not come with observation; nor will they say, 'See here!' or 'See there!' For indeed, the kingdom of God is within you.'"*
> Luke 17:20-21

The Kingdom within us is accessed by praise and thanksgiving.

David and Solomon were unquestionably mystics. They understood the spiritual world and what God was doing inside them. David strengthened himself in The Lord his God (1 Samuel 30:6). He knew where the Kingdom was: within him. The medium by which he entered God's Kingdom was by praising and thanking God.

> *"Enter into His gates with thanksgiving, And into His courts with praise. Be thankful to Him and bless His name."*
> Psalms 100:4

This strengthened his inner core. His mighty men and Solomon were taught and passed down the same principles.

> *"Now Solomon the son of David was strengthened in his kingdom, and the Lord his God was with him and exalted him exceedingly."*
> 2 Chronicles 1:1

Solomon was a type of Christ as the son of David in the Old Testament and Jesus Son of David in the New Testament. The Kingdom of God was within Solomon. Jesus told the Pharisees the same. He was strengthened from within.

The hand of the Lord means with the power of God, in other words supernatural speed force etc.

5. THE PURE AND SPOTLESS BRIDE OF CHRIST: A "BURNING ONE" ON FIRE FOR GOD. MORE ON THE BLOOD.

A post of praise:

I was woken one morning, in the middle of a dream where I heard the Lord saying:

"Jesus released His Kingdom to us through the sprinkling of His Blood."

The Old Testament Lamb that used to be slain had not opened up the Kingdom. The bride now needed to be spotless and pure. I wondered if this was referring to virginity and purity. The answer came back as a Big "Yes". He wanted to celebrate those brides who waited for their husbands and wives, and remained pure.

This part is praising and lifting up all women and men around the world today who await the bridegroom to release their earthly counterparts to them and who remain pure. They have withstood temptation, having faithfully prepared themselves for the lifting of their "veils". I do not need to go into detail as every woman knows what I mean.

At a wedding, the "husband-to-be" unveils His "bride-to-be" and enters the Holy of Holies. The wedding veil of a bride is light, soft and transparent. It is created to lift easily over the head to show Heaven and the Holy of Holies to the Bridegroom.

He gave the example of His Yoke in Matthew 11 v 28–30. It also is light and easy to bear. The old veil in the temple was thick and heavy. It needed lightning to break it. When Jesus died He split the Veil in the Holy of Holies. His body had to be torn and bloody for the veil to be broken.

> *"Therefore, brethren, having boldness to enter the Holiest by the blood of Jesus, by a new and living way which He consecrated for us, through the veil, that is, His flesh, and having a High Priest over the house of God."*
> Hebrews 10:19-21

Jesus' intention was always to make access to His Kingdom easy and light.

So, we have the intimate analogy beautifully replicated with the symbolic at a wedding and the supernatural where we can go through the veil into Heaven every day. As my brother Gary Beaton said in England some years back, "It feels like a true veil passing across your face as you enter the Realm that we came from."

But we need to work on being spotless and pure to enter Heaven regularly. We need to be "baptised", "by the refining Fire of Jesus" and become a Burning One. All precious stones and jewels are refined through fire.

Through Communion and the breaking of His Body (Bread) and acknowledging the Blood lost by Him, we get to become "intimate" with Him and similarly, this happens with Husband and Wife as the veil is torn and the bride experiences pain and blood. He told us He took the sins of the World and the "Brides-to-be" upon Himself so that when He returns, He has the absolute right to claim a Bride, Pure and Spotless.

We bless all men too who await their brides and remain abstinent...

6. BLASTED IN THE BRASSERIE — COMMUNION WITH THE SAINTS.

In the Brasserie Paul, opposite the Cathedral of Jean D'Arc in Rouen, we had an encounter with the young lady. She was medium height in a white robe. She had a squared-off fringe, and a belt around her waist. Her face seemed very ordinary but bright.

Standing at my left shoulder Elo saw her first. The young lady "said":

"I have been sent to help you.
As long as you need me, I'll be there.
You're going to need me to train up God's army.
Your wife is very brave.
I like to be around people with whom He can identify with.
I am here to give you a greater understanding that love is a weapon of war and gentleness is as powerful as the sword."
We were dealing with this while the owner served me a Virgin Mary, very appropriate. Then if we didn't have enough to cope with, Abraham turned up in full regalia and handed over first a

scarf then the Lord arrived giving a staff to him which in turn Abraham gave to me. It was like a shepherd's crook in style.

The Maitre D' looked at me waiting for me to order as I was in tears and totally blasted. My beloved on the other side of the table was not in any better state. We had just come out of this amazing cathedral glorifying the Lord of Lords. I had bought Elo, who carries her mantle, a pendant of the Maid of Orleans which she wore around her neck.

Jean D'Arc reminded us later that the communion held the same importance and power in our lives as it did in hers.

MORE REVELATIONS ON ONENESS AND COMMUNION WITH THE LORD

7. INTINCTION

While my beloved and I were taking communion one day, I was immersing the bread into the Wolfberry juice, when I got majorly "zapped" by the Holy Spirit. This is and should be a very Holy moment for all. The Lord spoke to me "My Blood must return into the Body..."

He said the bread is His body which is His Church. The wine which is His Blood is His DNA, and life in us. Our bodies do not function without blood. His Blood has to fill the body of the Church and us for it to be alive in Him.

> *"And they continued steadfastly in the apostles'*
> *doctrine and fellowship, in the breaking of bread,*
> *and in prayers.*
> Acts 2:42 (NKJV)

As Jesus is Water and Blood, we must immerse ourselves in the

River of Life and His Blood.

> *"This is He who came by water and blood—Jesus*
> *Christ; not only by water, but by water and blood.*
> *And it is the Spirit who bears witness, because the*
> *Spirit is truth."*
> 1 John 5:6 (NKJV)

There is only life in the Blood. Without blood flow, there is no life. Without river flow, the earth or ground becomes arid and dies. The Body of the Church won't function without us being immersed in His Blood. Our bodies won't function. The Church will not function without regular communion with Him. The Body and the Blood mixed and immersed together bring Oneness.

ARROW NINE
THE BAPTISMAL TRINITY

The Lord impressed upon me to add one more arrow. Nine represents the Holy Spirit and the gifts which are very appropriate for this arrow. It is an arrow of Power and Belief.

I had never realised that there were truly three baptisms: Water, Spirit and Fire. In many cases, a person can experience them one after the other or even over time.

Often the gift of spirit language or tongues is given to us immediately so we can commune with Heaven without any interference of Man. It is the supreme form of communication with God

The *Dunamis* power of God is brought to us by the Holy Spirit from Heaven to Earth. Yeshua was clear that He had to return to Heaven before the Father could send the Holy Spirit.

John the Baptist was very clear about his role as water baptiser. He clarified that Jesus would bring baptism by the Spirit and a baptism of Fire.

WATER BAPTISM

> *"I indeed baptize you with water unto repentance, but He who is coming after me is mightier than I, whose sandals I am not worthy to carry. He will baptize you with the Holy Spirit and fire."*
> Matthew 3:11

The water brings renewal by submersion, almost drowning the old life and bringing a new birth of life. As it says in the Bible, a seed must die in order for birth to happen.

BAPTISM OF THE HOLY SPIRIT

The Spirit brings the power of the Godhead into us. It is no surprise that people baptised in the Spirit are often impacted physically with jolts and quivers of electricity and energy. This is the toned-down power of the *Dunamis* that hovered and breathed over the cosmos to create all, entering us.

> *"But you shall receive power when the Holy Spirit has come upon you; and you shall be witnesses to Me in Jerusalem, and in all Judea and Samaria, and to the end of the earth."*
> Acts 1:8

The Lord would not want power and authority handed over where the vessel containing the Spirit was not perfectly clean

Often the gift of spirit language or tongues is given to us immediately so we can commune with Heaven without any interference of Man. It is the supreme form of communication with God.

With power comes powerful prayer that is wholly spirit. It is not a prayer to impress man but to commune with the Godhead spirit to Spirit.

> *"For he who speaks in a tongue does not speak to men but to God, for no one understands him; however, in the spirit he speaks mysteries."*
> 1 Corinthians 14:2

"And when you pray, you shall not be like the hypocrites. For they love to pray standing in the synagogues and on the corners of the streets, that they may be seen by men. Assuredly, I say to you, they have their reward. But you, when you pray, go into your room, and when you have shut your door, pray to your Father who is in the secret place; and your Father who sees in secret will reward you openly."
Matthew 6:5-6

FIRE BAPTISM

The Fire baptism is, I believe, the fiery heat and flames of the Seraphim angels touching us in order to purge us of anything evil remaining, purifying us as fire does. It refines us and cleanses us for the journey ahead.

The Lord would not want power and authority handed over where the vessel containing the Spirit was not perfectly clean. The wineskin parable shows one does not put new wine into an old wine skin. Here is the continuing verse from Matthew 3:11 that shows this purification and separation like the harvest with the tares and the wheat. The field is scorched with fire afterwards.

"His winnowing fan is in His hand, and He will thoroughly clean out His threshing floor, and gather His wheat into the barn; but He will burn up the chaff with unquenchable fire."
Matthew 3:12

No Father would hand over a loaded gun to a son who was not ready to use it.

The powerful gifts of the Spirit (walking in signs and wonders) are limitless in the hands of a true believer. As we bring Heaven to Earth, we are bringing the full force of the Triune Godhead through us.

This Anointing requires responsibility, humility and utter obedience and belief.

BELIEF

In order for one to operate in the gifts effectively, one needs belief and faith. The Lord asked us why the word "**Substance**" was used in the verse Hebrews 11 v 1.

> "Now faith is the substance of things hoped for, the evidence of things not seen."
> Hebrews 11:1

Upon research, it was clear the word "substance," embodied wholeness, totality, and completeness. So "faith" is complete wholeness, 100 per cent. It cannot be anything less. We were then reminded of these verses:

> *"And these signs will follow those who **believe**: In My name they will cast out demons; they will speak with new tongues; they will take up serpents; and if they drink anything deadly, it will by no means hurt them; they will lay hands on the sick, and they will recover."*
> Mark 16:17-18

The word that stuck out was the word "believe".

Those who do not believe or do not have faith cannot operate in the gifts of the Spirit effectively. If they try without belief, it is witchcraft and occultism. Jesus called the disciples a perverse generation.

No Father would hand over a loaded gun to a son who was not ready for it to use.

Faith is the substance, the understanding that we are operating from Heaven to Earth as a channel or conduit. It cannot fail if it is decreed in Heaven when coming to Earth.

He reminded us of the castigation of His disciples who had failed to exorcise and cure a child. They were faithless among other criticisms.

'So Jesus said to them, "Because of your unbelief; for assuredly, I say to you, if you have faith as a mustard seed, you will say to this mountain, 'Move from here to there,' and it will move; and nothing will be impossible for you.'
Matthew 17:20

Kenneth. E. Hagin who had an extraordinary healing ministry was corrected firmly by Jesus never to use the word "If" when praying, as it implied doubt and unbelief. The person would likely not be healed due to fear of failure. He was instructed just to declare the healing proof, not sowing doubt just in case the action did not work. Source: Book by Kenneth E. Hagin I believe in Visions. Chapter 3 "IF" The badge of doubt.

THE BOW
A RESTING FAITH - SHALOM

No Arrow can ever be fired without the Bow. It is the engine or flywheel that permits the arrows to fly. In all our walks, what do we need?

A Resting Faith. Without a firm belief in our abilities and that of our God, we are helpless.

Jesus continually tried to drive this message to His followers. The miracles occurred through Faith and Peace. The peace was a Heavenly Peace, not an earthly one.

SHALOM AND THE 39 STRIPES

The 39 stripes were paid for in advance by Yeshua.

Shalom — wholeness, peace, (Meshulem) paid for in advance.

I came into the living room this morning and found my beloved crying. She had been pressing into the Name of the Lord and was seeking counsel on the "shalom" that He provides. When she was very young, she had seen and heard Him crying out over and over again at the flagellation, not understanding what was going on.

The verses below were fed into her mind today:

> "But His form was without honour, failing beyond all men, a man being in calamity and knowing how to bear sickness; because his face is turned away, he was dishonoured and not esteemed. This one bears our sins and suffers pain for us, and we accounted him to be in trouble and calamity and ill-treatment. But he was wounded because of our acts of

lawlessness and has been weakened because of our sins; upon him was the discipline of our peace; by his bruise we were healed."
Isaiah 53:3-5 Septuagint

"He is despised and rejected by men,
A Man of sorrows and acquainted with grief.
And we hid, as it were, our faces from Him;
He was despised, and we did not esteem Him.
Surely He has borne our griefs
And carried our sorrows;
Yet we esteemed Him stricken,
Smitten by God, and afflicted.
But He was wounded for our transgressions,
He was bruised for our iniquities;
The chastisement for our peace was upon Him,
And by His stripes we are healed."
Isaiah 53:3-5 NKJV

The Septuagint, which He wanted us to use, is more powerful in translation Despised (not liked at all) is less powerful than dishonoured. He bore our sins not just grief.

His bruise meant black and blue in Hebrew. Four hundred and sixty- eight whip stripes. 39 blows of 12 flails are required for transgressing the laws according to the Mishna. A total of 468 stripes!

The reason why we can get His Peace, Shalom, is because of the punishment He received due for us, laid on Him. That's why we say the greeting "the Peace of the Lord be with you". We could never give each other our peace.

Elo was then reminded of a time in Cape Town when she was trying to sleep, and her mind was too active, agitated and confused to get into a state of rest. She saw in a vision a Jewish man in a white robe and red sash walking by and for no apparent reason being attacked to the head with a stick. At the time she did not realise it was Yeshua.

Elo then saw the verse below appear in front of her face and merge into the transpiring scene.

> *"Again, he sent them another servant, and at him*
> *they threw stones, wounded him in the head, and*
> *sent him away shamefully treated."*
> Mark 12:4

As she saw that, she felt peace in her head arrive. His chastisement brought her internal peace.

Sometimes when we worry about health and well-being for ourselves and others it is easy to forget what Yeshua went through to get rid of sin, sorrow and sickness and bring us peace and rest. From the time He was born, He felt everything He came across and saw in people.

Imagine that pain to carry.

If we don't learn to see and love people the way He does, we have failed Him and everything He did for us.

A Resting Faith. Without firm belief in our abilities and that of our God, we are helpless.

No half measures. So, men, it's ok to cry when you see the pain in others. It's a sign you are a little way along the road to understanding how He feels. Therefore, we need to be inside His Name as He is Peace. Outside we will never attain full Shalom.

As Elo, my Beloved, was pondering one day, she heard the word "El Shaddai".

Now He asked us to look at the Hebrew numerology of the word "shalom" and the Hebrew letter meanings:

Shin — 300 The breasted one, the El Shaddai, the all-sufficient One.
Lamed — 30 teaches.
Vav — 6 securities (nailing, own, securing).
Mem — 40 is the concealed truth of God (the letter, in this case, is stumah — closed).

The total number of the letters making Shalom come to 376. 376

Hz is the sound for peaceful sleep. The fundamental frequency of the shofar is 376 Hz. The all-sufficient One teaches us security through the concealed truth of God.

ONE THING IS NEEDED. RIGHTEOUSNESS, PEACE AND JOY

Positivity and happiness and joy.

The only single constant in my life is the goodness of God. It is this predictability that permits me to be positive about the future. I know that His plans for me and the world are better than anyone's.

> *I know that my heart can be deceived and forever*
> *needs His nurturing heart to keep me on His path.*
> Jeremiah 29:11

> *"The heart is deceitful above all things,*
> *And desperately wicked;*
> *Who can know it?*
> *I, the Lord, search the heart,*
> *I test the mind,*
> *Even to give every man according to his ways,*
> *According to the fruit of his doings."*
> Jeremiah 17:9-10

> "If you can keep your head when all about you are losing theirs and blaming it on you. If you can trust yourself when all men doubt you yet make allowance for their doubting too." The opening stanzas from the poem "IF" by Rudyard Kipling.

I am not alone, I am sure, wondering what is going on in the world at present, concerned and sad about the continued massive divide between rich and poor and the violence and hatred.

We watched a beautiful film the other night called the *Eagle Hunters* about Kazakh tribes in the steppes and their lifestyle. The true story centres around a young girl who learns about a man's sport and pursuit of hunting with eagles. The simplicity of their life whilst adapting to hardship and maintaining the sunniest of dispositions are a marked contrast to the West. Their faith in their god is uppermost in all they do. In the nearest "town" the tribal children weekly board and return home to their families on the weekend to help farm, hunt and cook.

We appear to have so much available here in the West, as Warren Buffett states in his newsletter to the shareholders of Berkshire Hathaway, "Our countries, especially the USA, have advanced so far in such a short time."

Paraphrased "From a standing start 240 years ago America's economic dynamism is nothing short of a miracle.":

75 million owner-occupied homes, 260 million vehicles, top medical centres, talent-filled universities, hyper-productive factories, an amassed wealth of $90 trillion. Heavy debt to finance the assets but even in default the asset passes hands.

"Money is always there but the pockets change." Gertrude Stein.

Four million US babies born every year entitled to a public education cost mostly at local level $150000 per baby which converts into $600 billion per year, about 3.5% of GDP. Extraordinary statistics.

Yet;

> "For what profit is it to a man if he gains the whole world, and loses his own soul? Or what will a man give in exchange for his soul? For the Son of Man will come in the glory of His Father with His angels, and then He will reward each according to his works."
> Matthew 16:26-27

But how positive is everyone? How happy are they? Without knowing Jesus none will be truly happy.

The Lord said to me one day, "My extending my hand of friendship through My Son, Jesus Christ, to humankind should be an indicator of just how valuable and loved they are to Me. Man without Me is nothing. But Man with Me has the potential to become everything."

What is this potential, to have everything?

Problem: We cannot take any of these above assets with us to Heaven after death. Clearly, these assets we acquire and focus on have little value to Him. They are temporary, fleeting pleasures and accoutrements.

The hill tribes in the third world live simply, often without electricity. Their outer clothing is made from furs. Their tribal and family units are strong and tradition is one of the most important features in their life. The Jewish faith embodies this with their feast and worship days remembering their history and God's goodness to them.

My life is dedicated to two areas:

1. My pursuit of knowing and loving Yeshua and having Him flow through me into loving my family first and "extended family".

2. Doing His will.

I will be judged by what works I have done for Him in my life, not by my status or wealth. I am a seeker of souls to redeem, ensuring everyone hears the "knock on the door and letting Him in". By His grace and love, He redeemed me, and my sole purpose is to witness that change and be one with God.

Being one with Him brings His fullness authority and power, not mine. This task makes me joyful and positive.

> *"I am the vine, you are the branches. He who abides in Me, and I in him, bears much fruit; for without Me you can do nothing."*
> John 15:5

BOOMING ONENESS

When you're not at rest; be worried:

> *"Let us therefore fear, lest, a promise being left us of entering into his rest, any of you should seem to come short of it."*
> Hebrews 4:1

We were led by the Lord today to search the meaning of "Evil report"

> *"Even those men that did bring up the evil report*
> *upon the land, died by the plague before the Lord."*
> Numbers 14:37

These were the guys who came back with Joshua and Caleb and concocted a report that effectively scared everybody into reacting and not going into the Promised Land.

The Pharisees and Sadducees were present when God the Father opened the Heavens and spoke over His Son.

> *"But when he saw many of the Pharisees and*
> *Sadducees come to his baptism, he said unto them,*
> *O generation of vipers, who hath warned you to flee*
> *from the wrath to come?"*
> Matthew 3 7

Yet they spoke evil reports of Him afterwards because they feared and were not at rest. They were jealous and hated Him.

God, like Israel (Jacob), had given His Son (represented by Joseph), his coat of many colours whom he loved more than his other sons. The sons of Jacob became jealous and ill at rest and gave evil reports of him.

His bruise meant black and blue in Hebrew. Four hundred and sixty eight whip stripes. 39 blows of 12 flails required for transgressing the laws according to the Mishna. 468!!!

So evil reporting brings judgement. Magnifying the giants over God brings repercussions.

We only have one thing to fear and that is to fear or be worried when we are not relaxed. He wants us always to enter into His Rest and look to Him. When we turn away from looking at Him, Giants overtake us.

When the apostles were fearful as Jesus slept, they did not enter His rest.

These passages all lead to faith and belief as only in Rest can one truly believe. The promised Land was God's promise to His people.

Jesus embodies and personifies the Promised Land and has promised eternal life and people continue to reject this because they reject Him from fear or unbelief. When we come out of Rest who is the Prince of Peace (Shalom), we risk coming into unbelief. (Read Hebrews 4:1-4)

> "For in him dwelleth all the fulness of the Godhead bodily."
> Colossians 2:9

The fullness of God was the Promised Land in the Old Testament. Jesus is the full embodiment of this. So when we ingest His Body, we ingest the Promised Land and it becomes a part of us. Remember the Giants were supposed to be bread and not feared.

> *"Only rebel not ye against the Lord, neither fear ye the people of the land; for they are bread for us: their defence is departed from them, and the Lord is with us: fear them not."*
> Numbers 14:9

We can only eat the Giants if we eat the Bread of Life. Take communion and conquer.

> *"And Jesus said unto them, I am the Bread of life: he that cometh to Me shall never hunger; and he that believeth on Me shall never thirst."*
> John 6:35

UNPREDICTABLE GOD BUT SEARCHING FOR REST

As the Summer weather arrives in the shape it chooses, I follow sites that give me meteorological prognostications and tidal and wave heights. Expectant of good winds and waves for surfing, windsurfing and kite surfing.

No amount of local knowledge or gut feel and years of sailing and being at sea gives me the confidence to know when I should be rushing to the beach.

Just as God confounds the wise in all we do, so He does in our leisure time too. The Holy Spirit blows in whatever direction it wishes, whenever. There is no point in being agitated or overly excited. One learns to go with the flow.

My beloved watches me as my mood changes to expectancy when signs indicate the heralding of a good surf height or wind level. She generously allows me a break away for an hour to go with the wind and water flow.

Sometimes a window opens, and one misses it because the lack of announcement or other focus made it impossible for one to be there. Life in the Spirit is the same. One needs to be in Shalom/ Rest, looking out for the small cloud like Elisha, gazing into the distance. Being, not doing.

When one is doing from a "Be" state, it is quite different from doing from a "do" state The task is easier and more relaxed and joyful. Doing stuff from a driven agitated state uses more energy and strength. The unpredictability of the Holy Spirit requires us to be very flexible not fettered by the ox goads or pressures of what we think we should be doing. When the time comes it is the right time. The sandals of Shalom to avoid contamination.

Old wine or old wineskin. Which is worse? We are supposed to be purified vessels. When we operate in the spirit under the instruction of the Holy Spirit our effectiveness is measured by our purity of soul/heart.

Operating with anger or any emotion other than *Ahava* love, we risk bringing chaos.

This is why when revelating or legislating with His authority, it must always come from Him. If it comes from our soul without the peace of the Holy of Holies inside His Name, we are liable to get counterattacks from the enemy that can hurt.

This is why the Armour of Light (Ephesians 6 10-18) is what it is: total protection. We stand with the sandals of Shalom so nothing can hurt us.

So, if you operate in the spirit, be sure you are a purified vessel/ wineskin which is able to take the fine and perfect wine and revelation of the Lord Jesus Christ. Don't be contaminated with earthly thoughts or actions.

PRACTISING THE PRESENCE OF GOD-SHALOM

You do not need to be down on your knees in church to have Him there. Get inside His Name, His Shalom with your soul. Learn to walk with Him like Enoch. Remember, everything comes from God.

Unfortunately, much of what is practised today is tainted, abused, and changed from God's plan. Transcendental meditation, astral projection, new age metaphysics etc. Why do those that practise it or did, seem to think it originated by someone other than God?

That's why we say greeting 'the Peace of the Lord be with you.' We could never give each other our peace.

The enemy can only copy as he too was created by God. New age is just a distortion of what God planned. Too many people practice the presence of everything that is not God: Suspicion, lack of peace, unbelief, doubt, fear and uncertainty all belongs to the enemy.

If you have any of these, I will ask you to let the Lord show you why you are not partnering with Him.

You will know if you are travelling in the Blood and with the Holy Spirit. You will know and start to decipher the Word if you have revelations from Wisdom and the Holy Spirit. It's because He trusts you.

Druids practise with power and have no authority. Witches and Satanists can perform dreadful supernatural activities because they are tapping into the wrong source of power. Their latent soul power permits it. Gurus and Hindus frequently levitate but not with His authority.

We met a Hindu convert to Christianity in South Africa who regularly levitated but the day he gave his life to Christ, he could do it no more. He was to d very clearly by His Saviour he would be allowed to only when he had learned to walk with God.

I cannot imagine how religious persons can live satisfied without the practice of the presence of GOD. "For my part I keep myself retired with Him in the depth of the centre of my soul as much as I can, and while I am so with Him, I fear nothing, but the least turning from Him is insupportable." Brother Lawrence

THE FULL MIGHTY

"You want the Full Mighty don't you?" He said to me some time back. Not the full Monty.

When I walk with the Lord during the day, I know He is there. It must have been like when the apostles went about their daily bread. You commune, but what you yearn for is the full-on Presence to arrive in your environment. In the workplace often in a ministry you know He knows how challenging it gets. Staying calm, loving, peaceful amid manifestation and fleshly behaviour.

We all need that solo time when one can bathe in Him and His overarching love. To refresh and recondition.

He said to me, "It's like when I just wanted to get away from everyone to be with my Father. To chew the cud and speak about challenges, issues, successes, and failures."

My beloved anc I were asked by the Lord to observe the Sabbath in as much as a Shalom way as possible. For me returning from work on a Friday night it takes time to wind down. It is a special time for us as we are so close and miss each other when we are not together. This is when I want the Full and All Mighty descending on me and my bride. My wedding ring has the following inscription:

"Be still, and know that I am God; I will be exalted among the nations, I will be exalted in the earth!"
Psalms 46:10 (NKJV)

"Let be and be still, and know (recognize and understand) that I am God. I will be exalted among the nations! I will be exalted in the earth!"
Psalms 46:10 (AMP)

Or my favourite;

"Relax, and know that I am God!
I will be exalted among the nations;
I will be exalted in the earth."
Psalms 46:10 (Septuagint)

We need time to exalt Him and that's when He exalts us.

EPILOGUE

In this manner, therefore, pray: Our Father in heaven,
Hallowed be Your name.
Your kingdom come.
Your will be done
On earth as it is in heaven.
Give us this day our daily bread. And forgive us our
debts, As we forgive our debtors. And do not lead us
into temptation, But deliver us from the evil one.
For Yours is the kingdom and the power and the
glory forever. Amen.
Matthew 6:9-13

On Earth as it is in Heaven. Everything has been formed before in Heaven and needs to be brought down from Heaven to change the Cosmos and Earth.

Our own marriage happened in heaven before it was allowed to happen on earth. All Kingdom marriages have occurred in this way. Some people are privileged to see this in the heavenlies. We are humbled to have experienced this and met the Living God.

To live the Christ-centred life we need to empty ourselves, become selfless with Him within us, humbled, servant-hearted, have clean hands, have a pure heart and be obedient to His Word. Yeshua only worked from Heaven to Earth. Listening seeing and obeying.

He told us recently, "In order for you to advance and attain the new levels that I have for you, as these new domains which are fully known to me but unknown to you, you have to unlearn and forget everything you have been taught before. New rules apply. You have to be humble enough to learn."

> *Jesus gave them this answer: "Very truly I tell you,*
> *the Son can do nothing by himself; he can do only*
> *what he sees his Father doing, because whatever the*
> *Father does the Son also does."*
> John 5:19.

We have to be doing the same as Jesus. We can only draw from Unseen resources.

> *"As for you, the anointing which you received from*
> *Him abides in you, and you have no need for anyone*
> *to teach you; but as His anointing teaches you about*
> *all things, and is true and is not a lie, and just as it*
> *has taught you, you abide in Him.*
> *Now, little children, abide in Him, so that when He*
> *appears, we may have confidence and not shrink*
> *away from Him in shame at His coming."*
> *1 John 2:27-28*

Whatever He is teaching you is what you are called to work at and pursue. You must be more and more hungry for God and His Presence to become a Christ-Man. Our forerunners starting with the Galilean fisherman and saints through history to the saints of today always wanted more and as a result, shone like the brightness of the sun leading people to the Messiah.

I hope you have learned what an amazing God we have and how much there is to learn and experience.

God reveals matters only to righteous people who pursue Him and remain close to Him. The anointing normally smearing with oil is a form of consecration He bestows on us to walk in His power and is only for His purpose and not ours. Another way of describing the anointing is the liquid Dunamis power which manifests through the Holy Spirit. The Presence and Power of God.

Many believers who have tasted the anointing lose it because they think it is theirs and all about them.

Remaining a beginner whether you are a mystic, a prophet, an apostle, an evangelist, a pastor, or just a humble follower of Christ is the best advice we can give. Blessings and Love in your pilgrimage.

ABOUT THE AUTHOR

Andrew Meyrick is a troubleshooter in the spirit and a professional troubleshooter in real life.

As a qualified chartered accountant with 40 years of experience as a CFO and CEO in major global corporations, Andrew has no intention of retiring and believes the word is a curse. He has been an ocean racer, an alpine ski racer and enjoys tennis, windsurfing and kite surfing. He also learned a few martial arts along the way.

After reaching near rock bottom when his first marriage ended in 2004, Andrew had an epiphany experience with the Lord. At this physical encounter with Yeshua, he was born again and baptised in Water, Spirit and Fire. After a tough pilgrimage of self-cleansing from 2004 to 2012, with the help of the Holy Spirit, he published his first book "Warriors of Love".

In 2013 Andrew met and married Elo, his beloved wife. The supernatural story of how they met is in the book. They have three children, Amarissa, Alexandra and Peter. The latter son was promised in 2014 by Yeshua and arrived in 2020. Andrew has three daughters from his first marriage, Gemma, Jessica and Maddy, and has six grandchildren so far.

Andrew and Elo live and work in Switzerland on assignment.

Seraph Creative
Heaven's Heart for Earth

Seraph Creative is a collective of artists, writers, theologians & illustrators who desire to see the body of Christ grow into full maturity, walking in their inheritance as Sons Of God on the Earth.

Sign up to our newsletter to know about the release of other exciting books.

Visit our website:

www.seraphcreative.org